Cancer Consolations: God's Tender Mercies

KATY CAMPBELL

WESTBOW
PRESS®
A DIVISION OF THOMAS NELSON
& ZONDERVAN

WestBow Press books may be ordered through booksellers or by contacting:

WestBow Press
A Division of Thomas Nelson & Zondervan
1663 Liberty Drive
Bloomington, IN 47403
www.westbowpress.com
1 (866) 928-1240

Scripture taken from the King James Version of the Bible.

ISBN: 978-1-9736-0145-6 (sc)
ISBN: 978-1-9736-0146-3 (hc)
ISBN: 978-1-9736-0144-9 (e)

Library of Congress Control Number: 2017913067

Print information available on the last page.

WestBow Press rev. date: 8/29/2017

Introduction

My dear reader, I want to share with you my purpose in writing this book. I want so much, by God's grace, to convey to you God's faithfulness during difficult times. Although bad things happen—sometimes so hard we feel we cannot bear the grief—God is faithful. And he is good, kind, and compassionate. Lamentations 3:22–23 means so much more to me now because I feel I have lived the truth of these verses: "It is of the LORD'S mercies that we are not consumed, because his compassions fail not. They are new every morning: great is thy faithfulness."

Please understand that I know what it is to be so broken you feel you can't keep living and breathing from the excruciating pain you feel—pain that is both physical and emotional. I know what it is to feel you're being ripped apart in every direction. I know what it is to feel so agonized that your heart hurts and feels like it's breaking, slowly and desperately, till you feel it must have torn in two. I've known tears of overwhelming sadness, pain, discouragement, and despair. But I also know that Jesus says, "Come unto me, all ye that labour and are heavy laden, and I will give you rest" (Matthew 11:28). The Lord *is* there during every second of every minute of every hour of every day. Not only does he say, "I will never leave thee nor forsake thee," (Hebrews 13:5c) he also promises he "will not fail thee" (Deuteronomy 31:6c, 8b). I have never known the Lord to fail me. Quite the contrary; I have seen the Lord give joy in the midst of pain. I have seen him give me blessings that were so personal and so kind that I felt reassurance I was not alone.

I can't wait to share with you the goodness of the Lord. I want you to experience with me the tender mercies of the Lord that I've so richly experienced and to be renewed in your faith and hope in Jesus Christ. At the end, I want you to be able to say with me, as my associate pastor quoted on the glorious day of my wedding, "But God, who is rich in mercy ..." (Ephesians 2:4a). So now let me tell you all about God's tender mercies.

1

Hair Today, Gone Tomorrow

> But the very hairs of your head are all
> numbered. (Matthew 10:30)

One common association people make with cancer is the patient losing all of his or her hair due to chemotherapy. Before I found out I had cancer, I was a cosmetologist, a hair stylist. Although I've never been considered *prissy*, I've loved doing hair ever since I can remember. So especially because I practically lived in hair because of my profession, I cared about my hair and what it looked like. I dreaded losing my straight, thick, blond locks. I knew I would be an ugly little bald specimen, especially with my thin face and somewhat sharp nose. So I committed this dread of mine to prayer. I begged the Lord to help me, and I told him that if there were any way he wouldn't mind allowing me to keep my hair, I would like to keep it. But as I've seen so many times in my life, the verses are true that say, "For my thoughts are not your thoughts, neither are your ways my ways, saith the LORD. For as the heavens are *higher* than the earth, so are my ways *higher* than your ways, and my thoughts than your thoughts" (Isaiah 55:8–9, my emphasis).

The Lord did let me keep a decent amount of hair on my head for a while. He graciously allowed me to transition into having straggly little strands that, for a long time, I couldn't bear to shave off. So where is this huge blessing? Oh, let me tell you all about it!

To preface this story, let me give you some background information. On August 6, 2011, at age twenty-five, I was diagnosed with non-Hodgkin's lymphoma. A few days later after having a lump on my neck biopsied, I found out the extent of my cancer. It was stage four. If cancer spreads to either the bones or an organ, it is categorized as stage four. Mine was in both. The doctors informed me that my cancer had already spread to the bones of my legs as well as throughout my spleen. Lymphoma is a blood cancer, which means it's systemic (in the bloodstream) and also settles into the lymph nodes. My results showed that my little body (five foot two and ninety-eight pounds) was alarmingly packed with cancer, and it was especially concentrated in my stomach and spleen. My spleen (which hides behind the ribs and is supposed to be the size of a fist) held so much cancer that it stretched from right below my ribs to the bottom of my stomach. You could literally see the outline of it through my skin. The test results also revealed that although my lymphoma had begun as a slow-growing form, somewhere along the way it had metastasized (or mutated or broken off) into a fast-growing cancer as well. Its rapid growth was wreaking devastating havoc on my body. We had to start aggressive chemotherapy immediately.

A couple weeks after my first chemo treatment, I moved in with my best friend, Laura, and her husband, Peter. I had previously been living at home with my family, but in this new arrangement, I had my own room. This new situation obviously provided me with more quiet living with a married couple rather than with a family of five. My boyfriend, Tyler, who is now my wonderful husband, had a job that allowed him to take as much time off from work as he needed to help take care of me.

The first time I lost a lot of hair, I experienced it as most cancer patients: I was washing my hair, and as I took down my hands from shampooing, I saw these huge, unnatural wads of my precious hair in my hands. I felt devastated. I quickly finished washing my hair and headed back to my bed. Ty found me there, and I was lying in a crumpled heap, crying my eyes out. He worriedly asked what was wrong, and I chokingly told him. And here comes my special, priceless blessing from the Lord. As I lay in bed (as all I could do was lie in bed, aside from using the restroom and sometimes being able to take a shower), Ty promptly took a small trash can and set it next to my bed. We started to talk, and as we talked, he gently ran his fingers through my hair. Whatever hair came out of my head, he placed into the trash can, and whatever hair stayed on my head remained there for the rest of that day. This became a daily ritual, with Ty carefully stroking my hair, taking the unpleasant task of my hair loss on himself while we either chitchatted or plunged into a heart-to-heart conversation. Thus, the Lord turned my horror of losing my hair into a beautiful memory. To this day, I still think back to those talk times, and I only remember it as a special, priceless blessing that I wouldn't trade for all the money in the world. The verse is true about the Lord, that "his tender mercies are over all his works" (Psalm 145:9b). What a blessed girl I was to lose my hair! Otherwise, I never would've experienced such a precious blessing.

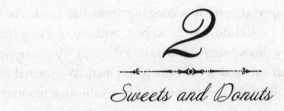

2

Sweets and Donuts

A merry heart doeth good like a medicine. (Proverbs 17:22a)

I have always had a ridiculously strong sweet tooth. I love candy, cake, ice cream, cookies, brownies—I think you get the point! I really had to become very careful about my sugar intake, though, because I believe that sugar feeds cancer (to some extent). Laura was really great about keeping my sweet tooth in check. But desperate times call for desperate measures, and I have some sweet memories that were a blessing to me.

Sweets

One of the biggest blessings I had regarding sweets revolved around Edy's frozen yogurt. I had had my first round of chemo and was still being hospitalized on account of how ill I was. I did have my good moments, however, and with those good moments came my cravings! The way my chemo affected me left me with little to no appetite. If I did have something of an appetite, it was only for one or two specific things. Anything else sounded gross. I might also add that my cravings didn't last long, so when I wanted something specific, I had a small window of time in which to eat it. Once that time frame expired, my desire to eat would be null and void.

My friend Rachel called me on her way to the hospital to visit me, asking if she could pick anything up for me. Happily for me, I really wanted some Edy's frozen yogurt! Being a devoted friend, she picked up the precious cargo and arrived with not only my yogurt but also another invaluable blessing—a visitor.

When I had cancer and chemo, I felt so unnaturally, dangerously ill that I couldn't even fathom what it would be like to feel better and normal again. In short, I felt like I would never get well. Oh, but the visitor! The Lord, in his tender mercy, knew what I needed for a huge burst of encouragement. Rachel brought her mother-in-law, who is a cancer survivor. I remember sitting on my hospital bed, eating my delicious frozen yogurt, and just staring at her healthy, normal-looking mother-in-law. She was happily eating and chatting away, telling me some of her experiences during her time with cancer. And yet this once sick, bald lady sat there with a head full of long hair, and she was functioning and completely alive and well. I really can't express the hope and happiness I felt from that visit. The Lord really used it to buoy my spirits. So my Edy's was sweet, but my "handful of purpose" (Ruth 2:16a) from the Lord was much sweeter!

Donuts

I will close out this sugary section with one more sweet story: donut devouring! As I mentioned earlier, Laura was outstanding about making sure I wasn't going nuts on the desserts. But one fateful, glorious night, she didn't get home in time to stop me. My sister, Kristen, and my friend Sarah came over to visit me. Like true pals, they came bearing a perfect Katy gift: a box of one dozen Krispy Kreme glazed doughnuts! I really had been doing well (for me, at least) at squelching my sweet tooth, so what could be more appropriate to celebrate my self-control than enjoying such gooey goodness? When Laura got home from the grocery store not much longer after they arrived, she found the guilty party (me) with the box of donuts in my lap, along with one donut in each hand. She gave me the "Katy-you-shouldn't-be-doing-that" look and said simply, "Oh, Katharine! No."

I looked at her with my guilty, somewhat remorseful eyes, half-full mouth, and full hands, and defended, "But they brought them for me!"

She shook her head and asked, "How many have you had?" I guess I had either put one of the donuts down, or eaten it very quickly, because I remember having a donut-free hand to answer. I silently held up three fingers, thus wordlessly confessing my sugar gluttony. She gave me a reproachful look and shook her head again. I didn't eat any more of those donuts.

Later that night, I was very sick from eating those marvelous three donuts, and I never did that again while I had cancer. But to this day, I still don't regret it. Hey, the Bible says "a merry heart doeth good like a medicine" (Proverbs 17:22a), and I was very happy!

3

A Survivor's Spectacular Advice

Blessed be God ... Who comforteth us ... that we
may be able to comfort them which are in any
trouble, by the comfort wherewith we ourselves
are comforted of God. (2 Corinthians 1:3–4)

Unless you've had personal experience with cancer (either
personally or through being with a friend or relative),
you don't know what to expect. Now they have classes,
at least for certain kinds of female cancers, to build support and
help you know what to expect. But I didn't have a female cancer,
and I didn't have time to attend classes (nor did I know of any)
before my chemotherapy treatments began. I had to start chemo
immediately. But the Lord sent me help, encouragement, and
advice right at the very beginning.

A young man in our church, Caleb, had had cancer several
years before. Although it hadn't been lymphoma, his cancer
required very aggressive chemo—just like mine did. I remember a
few days after my first chemo treatment, after my doctor released
me from the hospital, I went to church on Sunday. I thought, *Well,
I can either be in terrible pain and really ill at church or at home ...
I'd rather be at church.* I wanted to get encouraged in the Lord.

I remember feeling so sick, though, and being in so much pain,

I struggled to stay there through the sermon. But the Lord gave me a huge blessing from being there. After the service, Caleb caught my eye. When he looked at me, I saw instant recognition in his eyes. He understood! Somebody understood! I could tell he knew exactly what I was going through. He came over to me, made a sympathetic face, and said simply, "Feeling crummy?" All I could do was nod my head. "I know. It stinks," he replied.

He prayed with me and told me he'd keep praying for me. Then that was it—I had to leave. I couldn't even walk to the car by myself, I was so ill. But that short exchange meant the world to me. Just knowing and seeing someone else who'd gone through a harrowing experience with cancer and now lived a normal life, cured from that disease, provided me with an indescribable blessing. I wasn't the only one who'd gone through something like this!

He also gave Tyler invaluable advice for me. He told him to make sure I stayed on top of taking my pain medication. He elaborated that it's really tough to play catch up with the pain once it had set in. He also explained that it was important for me to stay cool and comfortable. He expounded that if I got too hot, I'd very quickly become overheated and therefore dehydrated, and that it'd make me really sick (I would throw up repeatedly).

So I took heed of his survivor advice, and it made an enormous difference! I noticed that everything he said was true. I know the Lord used Caleb's past experience with cancer to help make mine a little easier. Thank God for my survivor friend's advice! It spared me a great deal of misery. The Lord knew I wouldn't be able to attend cancer classes or support groups, so instead he graciously brought a mini class and support group to me. I'm so blessed to have the Lord in my life! He has always taken care of me like no one on earth can.

4

Angels Unawares?

Fear thou not; for I am with thee: be not dismayed;
for I am thy God: I will strengthen thee; yea, I will
help thee; yea, I will uphold thee with the right
hand of my righteousness. (Isaiah 41:10)

Have you ever met someone who just seemed to have
something special about him or her? Someone who
instantly set you at peace and at ease? I have, and I want
to tell you about him. My treatment plan called for not only
my regular intravenous chemotherapy treatments every three
weeks, but also four lumbar punctures (thank God I only ended
up having to get two). These lumbar punctures (LPs) were a
preventative measure against the cancer spreading into my spine.
This procedure consisted of a doctor first inserting a needle into
my spine and extracting some of my spinal fluid. He then took
another needle, also placing it in my spine, and injected chemo
into it. I felt absolutely petrified. I remember crying and praying,
praying and crying, and literally trembling when I thought about
this procedure. The fact that I was incredibly thin scared me even
more, because I thought it would probably cause the needle to
hurt a lot. (I don't know if, in reality, that's the case or not—I just
know it was part of my fear.)

9

The day for my first LP arrived. I remember that I had to go in alone. But in reality, I wasn't alone. I had the Lord right there with me to help me. And help me he did! A nurse wheeled me into the procedure room. There I sat, quietly and timidly in my wheelchair, with my Bible in my lap. Then I met my kind, special doctor. This doctor was an older man, probably in his sixties, with thick, comb-over gray hair and bushy, gray eyebrows. I remember that I instantly liked and trusted him. He saw my Bible and asked, "Do you want me to pray with you before we do the procedure?"

"Oh, yes!" I replied with great relief. He held my hand and prayed with me, asking the Lord to help everything go well. The nurse then helped me onto the table, which was tilted slightly upward toward the ceiling. As the doctor began sanitizing a spot next to my spine, the nurse held my hand. I concentrated on praying and breathing. Although the needle for the lidocaine (numbing) burned a little, the needle for the actual LP barely hurt at all.

After he finished, I had to lay flat on my back for the next hour. Sitting up too soon could cause a headache. I remember feeling so peaceful afterward, without experiencing an ounce of pain. The procedure had gone flawlessly—praise the Lord—with no complications whatsoever. A few days later my dad told my oncologist (cancer doctor), Dr. Collins, about the doctor who had performed the LP. He raved about what a great job he had done, and I agreed. Dr. Collins asked what his name was, and when my dad told her, she looked confused. She then asked for his physical description. As my dad described him, her brow furrowed more deeply. She answered, "I don't know anyone who works here by that name or that description, and I know the people who work in that department pretty well."

Well, whoever that guy was, he did an extraordinary job. He also prayed with me beforehand. So, to this day, I wonder if the Lord sent an angel there just for me. Either way, the Lord once again demonstrated his ability to take care of me. He can be trusted with and in any situation. He showed me such mercy in taking a situation that terrified me and taking care of every aspect perfectly. What a mighty God I serve!

5

This Little Piggy Went to Market

Rejoice evermore. (1 Thessalonians 5:16)

Have you, my dear reader, ever had a terribly horrible day when you felt so sick and miserable, you were sure nothing would or could make you feel better? I have. I remember one day early into the time I had cancer that was overwhelmingly awful. I had had my first chemo treatment, been hospitalized for several days, and then been sent home. Unfortunately, I stayed so ill at home that I would throw up until I was completely dehydrated. To try to rehydrate, I had to drink water. But if I drank water, I couldn't keep it down. Thus I became more dehydrated. It was a vicious and scary cycle.

On a good note, my doctor told me that the chemo goes in and kills the cancer tumors. When the tumors die, as gross as this will sound, they spit up their insides, thus releasing its toxins into your system. The result: throwing up. The bright side: the chemo is working and getting rid of the cancer tumors. This specific, nightmarish day, however, I didn't care about the fact that cancer tumors were dying and spitting up their insides. All I could focus on was me spitting up *my* insides.

Therefore, once again, I was off to the hospital to not only get fluids at the infusion center but also to get admitted into

12

the hospital again. The hospital didn't have any available rooms on the cancer floor yet, so I had to stay in the infusion center. I *hated* the infusion center. This center was a large room lined with recliner chairs. Cancer patients, as well as other patients, sat in these recliners to receive intravenous treatments. These treatments included receiving fluids, blood transfusions, chemo, and so forth. I always thought of the infusion center as a meat market, and all of us patients were the animals packed in and lined up for the slaughter. Those are dark thoughts, I know, but I just hated this room.

So this particularly depressing day, I remember sitting dejectedly in a recliner with my little throw-up trash can right beside me. I remember just staring off at nothing, sadly and miserably thinking, *Absolutely nothing can make me feel better.* My dear mom had called Tyler, telling him how sick I was, and that I was back at the hospital. My faithful man left work early and came to be with me. Even when I saw him, though, I just looked at him dismally and then hung my head down.

Now, my dear reader, if you have not yet discovered a pattern with the Lord and how he works, allow me to divulge it to you: the Lord allows very dark times to happen—dark enough that sometimes one can feel at the end of one's rope. But Jesus Christ promises his children, "My grace is *sufficient* for thee: for my strength is made perfect in weakness" (2 Corinthians 12:9b, my emphasis). He also promises, "Weeping may endure for a night, but joy cometh in the morning" (Psalm 30:5c). I have found that sometimes in life, you can feel very alone and stranded. You can feel like Peter did in the Bible, when he began to sink in the water from looking at the storm around him instead of looking at Jesus. But Jesus Christ was there the whole time and didn't let Peter drown. The Lord has never let me drown in my circumstances either in the storms of life. He has allowed me to suffer, sometimes what I felt was severely, but he has always rescued me. Such was the case on this desperately difficult day.

So in walked Tyler, and as I sat there with my head hanging down, he came over to me and knelt by my feet. Undaunted by my hollow state, he took my sandals off. He held one of my feet in his hands and began to wiggle my big toe: "This little piggy went to market," he explained, looking at me with mock seriousness. He moved on to my next toe: "This little piggy beat up this little piggy (the third toe was getting beat up by the second toe) because he wanted roast beef." Ty then began acting out a knock-down-drag-out fight between my toes, punching sounds included. Before I realized what had happened, I was first smiling and then soon giggling. He was just so funny with his silly little piggy rendition! Thus the Lord sent Ty to me to give me joy in the midst of my sorrow. Ty had said that on the way to the hospital, he had prayed the Lord would use him to cheer me up. The Lord really answers prayer!

So the part of this seemingly atrocious day that really stands out in my memory is my sweet Ty telling me the rightful "This Little Piggy" story—a story that caused me to laugh at a time when I thought laughter was impossible. It was yet another testament to God's faithfulness with his small but significant blessings at a time when I needed them most.

6

The Day of Small Things

For who hath despised the day of small things? (Zechariah 4:10a)

I have already mentioned that I hated the infusion center. The nurses were helpful and nice, but I just couldn't bring myself to enjoy sitting in a recliner while being hooked up to my chemotherapy. Also, the infusion center had several large TVs playing. The problem with this was that most of the TVs were either turned to a cooking channel or to a show about celebrities. Let me explain why this was a problem for me: cooking shows showcase food. But I was very ill, and almost all food looked sickening to me. Celebrity gossip channels showcase celebrities. These celebrities are shown posing while getting their pictures taken. Their hair, makeup, and clothes are perfect. Well, I didn't have much hair, and I was too sick to style it anyway. I didn't have the health or strength to put on makeup. As for clothes, I practically lived in my pajamas. That was the only type of clothing that felt comfortable. I remember watching the celebrities on TV and thinking, *They have no idea how blessed they are to be well enough to stand up and get their picture taken. And they're healthy enough to sit up in a chair long enough to get their hair and makeup done without getting sick.* Needless to say, watching those two channels made me feel very depressed because these were the thoughts that went through my mind. Plus, I was sitting in the meat market room, receiving my chemotherapy—a therapy that I knew would make me desperately ill by the next day. Ah, but the Bible says, "The LORD is gracious, and full of compassion … and of great mercy" (Psalm 145:8). Now I get to share with you my enormous blessing from the Lord—a blessing that came from my being so small.

One positive aspect about the infusion center was that it had wide recliners. They were big enough to fit about two-and-one-half of me onto them. I therefore had extra seating room. And from having this extra room, Tyler and I made a wonderful discovery: there was enough room for him to sit in the recliner with me! And he did! What an instant pick-me-up to this sad situation! So, from this discovery on, when I received my chemo (and later on, my blood transfusions), there we sat, happy as two bugs in a rug. I can't express to you how gigantic of a blessing this was to me. People would look at us and smile at how cute and special it was for us to share a seat, and I would beam back at them. My, how blessed I was to have someone I love so deeply *literally* be right by my side through such a tough circumstance!

I would also like to include one other small object that became a huge blessing: a portable DVD player! For my first chemo treatment (my doctor hospitalized me for my first and second round), Ty bought a small, portable DVD player for me. That little gadget turned out to be a godsend for the whole duration of my cancer! It was wonderful to have in the hospital during all of my hospitalization bouts, and it also came with me to all of my chemo sessions. So, after my first chemo session in the infusion center with those abominable TV shows, we brought along the DVD player and put in movies of our choice. It was like our own personal little movie theatre. No more being subjected to those upsetting TV channels!

Ty told me he believed the Lord put it in his heart to get that DVD player for me. He had no idea how helpful and important it was going to be for me, but the Lord did! I truly believe that the Lord, who knows the end from the beginning, was mercifully and graciously looking out for me. He provided for my needs before I even knew what they were! Praise the Lord! I believe the Bible sums these blessings up perfectly: "For who hath despised the day of small things?" (Zechariah 4:10a). I have two tiny words for you: not me!

7

Barren

But Sarai was barren; she had no child. (Genesis 11:30)

I understand what it's like to have a lifelong dream in place, only
to receive horrible news that tears it from you in a matter of
minutes. The shock and devastation is terrible—and so sad. Let
me tell you what happened to me, and tell you how God worked
a blessing in the midst of a dark message.

My cancer was very aggressive, and therefore, my chemo had to
be too. I was lying in my hospital bed on Monday, August 16, 2011,
with my family (my dad, mom, sister, Kristen, and brother, Jeremy)
and Tyler in the room with me. My oncologist, Dr. Collins, was
explaining to me that I had a slow-growing cancer that had been
present for at least six months to one year. But this slow-growing
cancer had metastasized, or broken off, into a fast-growing cancer
as well. She said we had to do chemo right away. And then the next
words out of her mouth riveted me with a piercing heartache. "I
need to tell you that this chemotherapy will make it so you won't
be able to have children." I remember feeling my heart drop to the
floor. I never expected to hear those words. She went on to say,
"We usually try to harvest eggs and save them, but I don't feel
comfortable doing that with you. Based on the way your stomach
feels from Friday to today, we don't have time."

Oh, I remember looking at her, nodding my head, trying to be strong. But then my eyes began to well with tears. I dropped my head, put my hand over my eyes, and began to cry. And then I began to sob. I loved kids and always wanted a small tribe of them. Yet there I sat, twenty-five years old, being told I would be barren. And what about Ty? I knew he loved kids too, and that it was a big deal to him to have them. This couldn't be happening! But it was.

Dr. Collins tried to comfort me, telling me if God wanted me to have kids, he could make it happen. I knew she was right, but what about Tyler? I didn't want him to feel obligated to stay with me, someone who almost certainly couldn't give him children. And yet, how could I live without him? No matter what the consequences, I had to talk to him.

Dr. Collins left the room, along with everyone else except my brother. I asked him to step out for a minute, and when he did, I turned toward Tyler and locked eyes with him.

"Look," I began. "I know what she said about my not being able to have kids is a big deal, and I want you to know that you don't have to stay with me, okay? I completely understand."

He just looked back at me and responded, "What do you mean I don't have to be with you? Are you crazy? It's the Lord's will for us to be together, and if he wants us to have kids, then we'll have kids. And if he doesn't want us to have kids, then praise the Lord. He knows best. You're not getting rid of me that easy!" And then he smiled at me.

More tears welled up in my eyes as I continued to look at him. I smiled back at him through my tears, choked out, "Okay, thanks," and then broke down crying again. Only this time, my tears were tears of joy and thankfulness. The Lord was giving me such a perfect guy and an incredible blessing from a painful situation. How many people, before they get married, are able to see that kind of character in a person? That kind of love, devotion, and conviction that is so rare today? I'll tell you who: a girl who was blessed with cancer, blessed with being told she couldn't have kids, because she got to see what kind of a man the Lord had sent her.

8

My Doctor from the Lord

Commit thy way unto the LORD; trust also in him;
and he shall bring it to pass. (Psalm 37:5)

A very important, and even life-changing aspect for a cancer patient is his or her doctor. My family, Tyler, my church family, and I prayed for just the right doctor for me. When I was in the hospital recovering from my biopsy, I met one of the oncologists. The oncologist, who I didn't know at the time, was to be assigned to me. I'll call him Dr. Warren. He spoke softly and seemed nice, but I didn't feel at ease with him. After all, this situation wasn't like I was going to a doctor to get an antibiotic for a cold. My life, to a large extent, was in his hands.

About two hours later, another doctor entered my room. I'll name him Dr. Herman. I was so groggy from the pain medication, I could barely answer his questions. Tyler, who was in the room with me, actually answered most of his questions. Once he was done with his lopsided conversation, he left his card with me and exited my room. That evening, my medication had worn off a lot, and a nurse came in to renew my dose. I don't remember her name, but I do remember that she was absolutely wonderful—and a godsend. I asked her how her day had been, and we chitchatted for a little while. As she was about to leave my room, I impulsively asked, "By the way, do you know Dr. Herman? He gave me his card."

"Oh yeah," she answered.

I then whispered, "Is he good? Do you like him?" Of course I assumed he was a good doctor—I just wanted some reassurance.

"Yup," she replied as she slowly nodded her head. Then all of a sudden, she shook her head "no," walked toward my door, and closed it all the way so no one could hear what she was going to say. She then explained, "I wouldn't want him. He's good, but not very compassionate and doesn't have a good bedside manner. A lot of patients complain about him."

"Oh!" I answered, my eyes as big as saucers.

She continued, "You want Dr. Carletta Collins. She's a young doctor, but very knowledgeable and aggressive toward cancer. She's also really compassionate toward her patients, and you two share the same faith. I've even seen her pray with her patients. If it were my sister or mom who was sick, that's who I would tell them to have."

I looked at her, not really knowing what to say. I finally questioned, "But haven't they already assigned my doctor to me?"

Her next words were both true and invaluable: *"You're* the patient, and you have the right to request whichever doctor you want. Just tell them someone recommended Dr. Collins to you, and that you want her to be your oncologist. They'll probably try to get you to stick with the original doctor they assigned to you, but it's your decision. It's your right as the patient to have who you want," she reiterated.

My dear reader, I look back on that day and am completely convinced that the Lord ordained that conversation to take place. That one off-handed question literally affected my whole cancer experience, and affected it for the better. I had unsuspectingly asked about her thoughts on Dr. Herman, not even considering that he wouldn't be a good fit. And Dr. Herman wouldn't have even been my doctor—Dr. Warren would've been. But neither of them was Dr. Collins.

I called and requested Dr. Collins, and although I had to wait a few days to get in with her, it was well worth the wait. I really believe that our doctor/patient rapport was a match made in heaven. She was absolutely perfect for me. Let me tell you just how perfect.

When I met her, she was very kind and friendly. She thoroughly answered all the questions I had. Furthermore, she customized my treatment to my specific case. Since I had a fast-growing cancer, she gave me very aggressive chemo (the dose/amount was aggressive). But she also *listened* to me as a person. She never just brushed me off as an imbecile when I talked to her about complaints I had. For example, the standard treatment for non-Hodgkin's lymphoma is CHOP-R. Each letter is the first initial to the name of a chemical. I was *so* ill after my first two treatments that she decreased the amount of two of the chemicals by 30 percent. Believe me, I was overwhelmingly thankful to her. (I later found out that Dr. Herman always went by the book, regardless of how ill his patients became. He never deviated, and that type of decision making probably would've been fatal for me).

She also told me that she prayed over what to do concerning every decision she made for each patient. Well, I trust the Lord, and I know that if one of his children asks him for wisdom, he'll give it to them. It's one of his "exceeding great and precious promises" to do so (2 Peter 1:4a). James 1:5 says, "If any of you lack wisdom, let him ask of God, that giveth to all men liberally, and upbraideth not; and it shall be given him." I know the Lord gave her special wisdom in her decision-making for my case. When I continued to stay horribly ill from my treatments, she omitted one of the chemicals altogether. I'm so glad she deviated! I got down to seventy-eight pounds (my starting weight had been one hundred and seven, at least nine pounds of which was purely cancer tumors) in the hospital, and I really believe the Lord used her careful, prayerful decisions to help save my life.

I could easily go on and on about her. She became more than just a doctor to me—I considered her a friend too. Her kindness, care, and competency were lifesaving blessings straight from God himself. In short, she was my doctor from the Lord.

9

Kids and Family—Blockbuster, Here We Come!

But my God shall supply all your need according to his riches in glory by Christ Jesus. (Philippians 4:19)

As I mentioned in the previous section, I had aggressive chemo that made me very ill. So ill, in fact, that I stayed bedridden. Needless to say, some entertainment to help pass the time helped immensely. Although I love to read, my chemo made it so that I couldn't concentrate on reading anything. It took too much effort. I tried to read at least one chapter of my Bible every day, and I listened to the Bible being read on CD a lot too. But, I also needed something to take my mind off of feeling so sick and being in such great pain. The biggest help: watching movies! I don't like to spend a lot of time in front of the TV, as I feel it robs people of time and brain cells. But I think you'll agree with me, my dear reader, that this counted as an extenuating circumstance! And if you're going to watch movies over the course of several months, you need some variety! After all, there were only so many times I could deal with *Anne of Green Gables* and *Secretariat*. Besides, poor Tyler watched all my movies with me. He stayed by my side, like a trooper, keeping me company. If

I couldn't deal with those two movies, he *certainly* couldn't, either! I normally enjoy action movies, but since I felt so sick, those types of movies were just too heavy for me. I had no desire to watch people fighting and getting shot. Plus, watching people run from bad guys made me even more tired. So all I could handle were very light movies. We rented movies and thankfully had a Blockbuster a few minutes down the road. But renting movies, especially at Blockbuster, is very expensive. So how could I possibly afford all these movie rentals? Let me tell you, my dear reader, the Lord truly cares about little details as well as big details. In his loving kindness, the Lord worked out a perfect situation for my possible movie dilemma.

Blockbuster just so happened to be having a special during the entire time of my cancer. For ten dollars a month, you could rent any two movies at a time from the "Kids and Family" section. You could switch these movies out as often as you pleased. My caring Ty faithfully went to Blockbuster, constantly switching out our movies. He had good taste, too, in the movies he picked out. We definitely exhausted the "Kids and Family" section, but praise God, it was an indescribable blessing to have all those movies available. The Lord knew exactly what I needed and when I needed it. Praise the Lord for him being true to his promises in his word. He truly did "supply all my need" (Philippians 4:19), and I am so very thankful to him for his perfect provision.

10

Card Consolations

Heaviness in the heart of man maketh it stoop: but
a good word maketh it glad. (Proverbs 12:25)

I think there is something very special about getting something personal in the mail. Especially if that something is handwritten and personally addressed to you. To be honest, dear reader, some of my time during cancer felt very dismal. But the Lord was so faithful in giving me encouragement when I needed it most.

During my first few months of cancer, people flooded me with "Get Well Soon" cards. These cards served as a tremendous source of encouragement. Individuals, couples, and families from all over the country sent me supportive mail, telling me they were praying for me and thinking of me. What a comfort to know that I wasn't going through this difficult time isolated and forgotten. Quite the opposite. I still feel so touched thinking about the thoughtfulness of others. Sometimes these cards hailed from people I knew but had lost contact with over the years. What a joy to hear from them again! Other cards arrived from people I didn't know who took time out of their busy schedules to encourage a stranger in need of kind words. Several times these cards reduced me to tears of gratitude.

As a Christian, I truly believe, as the Bible says, that you enter into a very special family—a family of believers that has a love and connection through Jesus Christ. This bond results in an instant friendship and closeness—a unity. You find people with whom you have something (a belief) and someone (Jesus Christ) very dear in common. You share the same Spirit, the Holy Spirit. Jesus said that once you have asked him to come into your heart to be your personal Savior (Acts 16:31a; Ephesians 2:8–9; Romans 10:9–10 KJV), he sends his Holy Spirit to live inside you (Ephesians 1:13). So, in addition to having the Lord with me every step of the way, he also gave me a sense of companionship with others in my spiritual family.

The Lord also provided a very specific family who served as tremendous card consolation people: Tyler's family. My dear future mom, dad, sister, and two brothers-in-law faithfully sent me one card every single day during the time I had cancer. On Tuesday, I received two cards: Sunday and Monday's. They signed these cards with sweet, short messages, saying they missed me, loved me, were praying for me, and hoped I had a good day. If they heard that I had had a particularly rough day or week, they empathized, saying they were sorry I felt so bad and that they hoped I was feeling better. Who does things like that, unfailingly sending a card every day? I'll tell you who: very loving, caring people, who, to this day, are a wonderful extended family to me.

Once again, what a mixed blessing the Lord gave me in allowing me to have cancer. Had he never allowed me to go through that trial, I never would have experienced the love and support that people from all over the globe extended to me. I feel so blessed.

11

Texting Tori: The Lonely Hours

And as you would that men should do to you,
do ye also to them likewise. (Luke 6:31)

Ty attended Bible classes (as he was in his second year of Bible school) Monday through Thursday evenings. I admired and still admire the strength of character the Lord gave him to stay faithful to what he called him to do. Ty knew the Lord had brought him to Florida from Colorado to attend Bible school. He had prayed about whether or not to drop out of school to help take care of me more, but he didn't feel peace about it. So, by God's grace, he continued with his classes. But that meant that for me, there were many an evening that I laid in bed, watching the clock slowly tick away the minutes. Those four hours felt like an eternity and were often very lonely.

But Tori, my future sister-in-law, got wind of my loneliness and brightened many of my nights. She began texting me during those hours, faithfully keeping me company. I have never forgotten those precious conversations. She really was a great companion, all the way from Colorado. She was always sweet, fun, and upbeat—and sympathetic, when needed. I don't know if she realized it, but our texting talks also marked a new experience in my life. At twenty-five years of age, all I had ever owned was a pay-as-you-go cell phone. And this phone was not a flat rate per month for unlimited talk and text. No, mine was one cent per minute, and five cents per one page of text, coming or going. I bought minutes in $100 card increments. This had been my practice since I was nineteen. Then, one glorious day, during cancer, my dad bought me a Verizon phone. This phone cost $50 per month for unlimited talk and text. Now this was a price I could afford! So, for the first time in my life, I could text freely, without cringing over every precious text.

During these texting hours, Tori and I talked about trivial things, and sometimes more serious things. During our talks, the time passed by so much more pleasantly. I have never forgotten those priceless conversations, and still have almost all her texts on that phone. I cannot do justice to express, dear reader, the extent of encouragement and help those refreshing texting torrents gave me. I'm so glad, to this day, that Tori was my breakthrough texting buddy! The Lord gave me yet another bright spot in the midst of a dark time.

12

Fight Night

Not forsaking the assembling of ourselves
together. (Hebrews 10:25a)

I have always enjoyed watching UFC (Ultimate Fighting Championship), and strangely, given my lack of desire to watch action movies while being so ill, that enjoyment of watching UFC continued during cancer. But a couple of problems presented themselves: not only was it hard to find a restaurant that played UFC fight nights, but I was also nowhere near well enough to sit in a booth or hard chair for all those hours. But I have seen that the Lord grants his children the most specific of blessings. For me, UFC was one such blessing.

I rarely left the house during cancer because I was too ill to do much of anything. But being so isolated at home became very difficult, especially since my personality is normally that of a social butterfly. I remember feeling so overwhelmingly frustrated with my limited existence. All I could do effectively was lay around and watch movies. I hated that so much. But the Lord hadn't forgotten me. He allowed me to stretch my wings from my little cubby by generously providing fight night.

A couple in our church, Dean and Shelly, also loved to watch UFC. Before my cancer, Ty and I attended fight night, where a small group gathered at their house and watched these hopefully epic fights. Over time, for whatever reason, fight night had dwindled. But kind Dean and Shelly remembered our love of UFC. So, they offered, to my extreme elation, for us to come over again to enjoy several fight nights with them. The set up was ideal: Tyler and I sat on the couch, where I could be comfy, lean back, and relax. This way I could still rest (sometimes falling asleep), and not fade out (have to go home) before all the fights were done. And, I must add, I felt so thankful to extend my social arena. Dean and Shelly's kids, Cassandra and Dominic, watched the fights with us, along with their cats and dog. Everybody (animals included) was great company.

As a group, we knew which fighters we wanted to win. And, being a rather vocal person with sports, I kept finding myself sitting upright, perched on the edge of the couch, cheering for our guy to "Get him! Get him! Yes! Put him down!" So there I sat, happily watching the fighters exchange kicks, punches, and grappling moves. I sometimes felt very pleased with myself when I could identify a jiu-jitsu move, such as an arm bar, kimura, rear naked choke, etc. Tyler loves Brazilian jiu-jitsu, so that's how I learned to identify some of the specifics. I also loved when our fighter won by TKO (technical knockout). Ty told me his old boxing coach used to say, "Everybody has a button, and when you hit it, his lights go out." I never liked the fights to get too bloody, though. If a fight did get too bloody, I just looked away until it was over.

Watching UFC at their house was a very big highlight for me during cancer. I enjoyed every minute of it, and also relished the rare opportunity to be out of the house. I learned to be very thankful for the blessing of being able to sit on a couch, happily watch the fights, and not take such a seemingly simple outing for granted.

13

Laura the Loyal

A friend loveth at all times. (Proverbs 17:17a)

True, loyal, loving friends are hard to find. I've heard that if you have one such friend in this lifetime, (besides the Lord), you've found a treasure. My dear friend Laura is just such a treasure. In Proverbs, the Bible says, "A friend loveth at <u>all</u> times" (Proverbs 17:17a), and she truly did. I honestly cannot express to you, my dear reader, the extent of love and gratitude I have for Laura. I know she is one of the main people the Lord used to literally save my life.

She spent the night with me at the hospital several times during the first part of my cancer. One night at the hospital, about two weeks after my first round of chemo, she made an unbelievably sacrificial offer. She saw how sick I was, and she knew that my family and I lived in somewhat small living quarters. As I mentioned in a previous section, I shared a room with my sister, Kristen. Although I had no complaints about her as my roommate, it's better for someone who's sick with cancer to have his or her own room. It provides more quiet and privacy. Laura realized this, having been in the medical field. So, she told me that if I ever needed a place to stay, she and her husband, Peter, would be glad to take me in. She explained, "You'd have your own room, and since I don't work, I'd be home and could take care of you. You wouldn't have to worry about paying us anything for living with us, either. We'll take care of it." I remember sitting in my hospital bed, utterly and completely stunned. What a kind, selfless offer! Of course I couldn't accept, but I felt so grateful for her willingness!

Well, the Lord had other plans. The very next day, my brother came down with a fever and a stomach virus, making it impossible for me to go home (I was about to be discharged from the hospital). So, after explaining the proposal to my family, off I went with Laura to her home. The living arrangement became permanent until I got married. Thus I became a new member of their wonderful home.

When I entered my new room, the bed was made, with an adorable little stuffed monkey sitting on it. He looked so friendly and inviting. I had never had my own room before, either. It was like Christmas for this cancer patient! I quoted the verse earlier about "a friend loveth at all times." And I promise you, my dear reader, no friend could ever show more love than she did. She cooked and brought me breakfast, lunch, and dinner. My organized friend also kept track of when I needed to take my medicine (pain killers, anti-nausea, etc.), and made sure I never missed a dose. On top of all that, she dealt daily with having an extremely sick person living in her home. I was so ill, in fact, that my oncologist once told me that I was her sickest patient. So you can only imagine how ill I was and how weighty of a situation Laura dealt with. But she never, ever complained about taking care of me, nor did she ever make me feel guilty about being there. Not once did she cause me to feel embarrassed or gross by how much I threw up. And especially during the first couple of months of cancer, I threw up at least twenty times a day. She just put a bucket next to my bed, and, acting as if cleaning up your friend's throw-up was the most normal thing in the world, she faithfully and nonchalantly took the bucket, cleaned it out, and placed it beside my bed again. I couldn't have had a more kind, attentive friend. What a blessed girl I am to have had her taking care of me!

She was also wonderful company! When Ty couldn't be there, she trooped herself into my room, sat down on my bed, and hung out with me—sometimes for hours at a time. We talked, laughed, reminisced, and watched Hallmark movies. The Lord used her friendship and support to carry me through an extremely difficult, turbulent time. In more ways than I can express to you, my dear reader, she saved my life, and I feel I can't do justice to describe how much she meant and still means to me. God is so good to give me such a loving, faithful friend. Thank God for such a terrible illness that allowed me to see how rich the Lord's blessings are, in even the worst situations. He gave me Laura, and he showed me what a priceless blessing it is to have a friend that "loveth at all times."

14

Aunt Joyce the Voice: Telephone Talks

A word spoken in due season, how good is it! (Proverbs 15:23b)

When I found out I had cancer, I didn't really have any close cancer buddies in Florida to compare notes with about how I was feeling. I didn't know what to expect as far as how ill I would be or what were considered normal symptoms in the chemo arena. But my faithful, loving Lord graciously filled that void and gave me the perfect go-to person: my dear Aunt Joyce. My aunt had had cancer a few years before me. Although we didn't have the same type of cancer, we did have something very important in common: genetics.

As soon as she found out I had cancer, she called my hospital room to see how I was doing. Tyler explained my diagnosis, and, after the first few weeks where I was too ill to talk on the phone, my aunt became my almost daily talking buddy throughout the months I battled this difficult disease. She not only helped and encouraged me tremendously, but also became a close friend.

She told me all about her experience with cancer, which, before that time, I had never heard in full detail. Oh, but what a help those details were! Finally I found someone who understood firsthand the physical and emotional struggle that goes with chemo and cancer: the pain, weakness, indescribable fatigue, sickness, frustration, and discouragement. We had many heart-to-hearts about issues I dealt with emotionally, and I believe that the Lord, over and over again, gave her just the right words to help me. I can also say the same for the physical aspects. The Lord used her to be an oasis in a very dry time in my life.

We also shared lots of laughs and fun talks too. She was currently enrolled in college again to get her master's degree, so even getting to chat about something aside from my cancer provided a huge help. We discussed memories from years back, old movies we liked, and much more. What an indescribable blessing and help the Lord provided for me in my Aunt Joyce. Our talks served as a help I didn't realize I needed so badly. Thank God for my Aunt Joyce's voice and our telephone talks.

15

Sixty Minutes

And as thy days, so shall thy strength be. (Deuteronomy 33:25b)

During cancer, I experienced many ups and downs. I could go from feeling encouraged one day to feeling very discouraged the next—or vice versa. Sometimes these mood changes occurred in the same day: one portion of the day could be bad, while another portion turned out to be quite good. Later I found out that one of the chemicals in my chemotherapy regimen actually caused chemically induced depression. And those times when depression hit were pretty awful.

I remember going through a segment of time when I felt particularly down. I was sick of being sick, sick of being bedridden, sick of feeling like I had such a wasted existence. I prayed for the Lord to help and encourage me—to give me some relief. And the Lord, in his tender mercy, did just that. He sent me some visitors who brought a bright spot to what had been a very despondent day. These visitors, who are evangelists, were the Spurgeons. Brother Dave Spurgeon, Mrs. Sue Spurgeon, and their daughter, Evay, stopped by for an unexpected visit. Tyler and his family had been really close friends with the Spurgeons for years. Brother Spurgeon had preached a youth camp I had attended one summer, and also preached for a couple of different revival services at my church in Pensacola, Florida. Then, when Tyler and I were in the very beginning of our relationship, I had the blessing and privilege of getting to know them on a more personal level. I loved them! And now, about a year and a half later, the three of them came trooping into my lonely room for a visit.

We talked about historical sites they had seen while traveling the country (I love history, as that was my major in college), as well as their experiences in Canada, England, and Scotland. Evay imitated a very authentic-sounding Scottish accent for me, along with a killer Boston accent, which I found quite entertaining. They visited with me for about an hour, and the time flew by! I remember feeling so cheerful, encouraged, and just plain happy with them. They left all too soon, and I remember actually feeling deflated when they were gone. But I'm still so thankful to the Lord for their visit. It provided me with an hour that was so uplifting, and I've never forgotten what a difference it made for me. The Lord also used those precious sixty minutes to teach me an invaluable life lesson: sometimes the Lord allows us to go through very hard times. And sometimes those hardships last for a more extended period of time than we want. But it's so important to always be thankful (1 Thessalonians 5:18a: "In everything give thanks") and to count your blessings (1 Thessalonians 5:16: "Rejoice evermore"). If it's been a bad day, well, it makes your good days that much better. In the case of a harrowing illness, where there seems to be a lot of tough days, then break those days down into smaller increments. For example, maybe you had a really bad, difficult, painful, sick hour. Okay, fine. Then maybe the next hour will be better. Or even the next five minutes will be five minutes of some relief. That kind of mindset, I have found, makes a world of difference in how you either will or won't enjoy life. And that day the Spurgeons visited me, the Lord gave me a wonderful sixty minutes—sixty minutes of happiness instead of sadness; sixty minutes of relief instead of sixty minutes of pain. And to this day, I'm so thankful for them.

IV Explosion

For God hath not given us the spirit of fear; but of power,
and of love, and of a sound mind. (2 Timothy 1:7)

My first time being hospitalized happened the night I found out I had cancer. My friend Rachel stayed with me, offering great support. I had so many people praying for me, I can honestly say I didn't have a bad night. The Lord gave me his "peace that passeth all understanding" (Philippians 4:7), and I slept well.

The next day, however, held some challenges. The ER doctors decided to take a biopsy from one of the two lumps on my neck. Although I felt very afraid about having a surgeon slice into the left side of my neck, the Lord provided an excellent surgeon. She didn't slip and slice open my jugular vein, much to my relief, and I came out of the surgery with flying colors. Praise the Lord!

Later that night, however, my uneventful experience changed. One thing I realized during cancer was that something can happen that's not an earth-shattering crisis, but it's an experience that takes the wind out of your sails. Such was my experience that night.

I was in my hospital room, complete with a not-so-flattering hospital gown, a long white patch taped on the side of my neck, and an IV tube strung from my arm to the IV machine. My friends

Laura, Stephanie, and Dana were visiting me, along with Ty, my dad, and my brother, Jeremy. We were having a good time until I got up to wash my hands. I had to tote my IV machine, which I nicknamed "Linus," with me. (The nickname came from the character Linus in *Peanuts*. Linus carried his blanket with him everywhere he went, just as I dragged my IV stand with me everywhere I went. So, the name seemed to be a perfect fit.)

I entered the bathroom, and then I felt a slight snap in my arm. I looked down to see blood spurting out everywhere from my IV tube. One of the attachments had broken off.

I yelled, "Guys! Guys!" One of my friends ran into the bathroom, only to stop short, stare, and run straight back out at the sight of blood shooting all over the room (a completely understandable reaction). Then in rushed Ty, and quick as a flash, once he surveyed my problematic IV, took his index finger and covered the opening. Instantly, the mini blood explosion ceased. A nurse came in a minute later and fixed the attachment.

After the excitement calmed, I remember I slowly sat down on my bed and hung my head. I suddenly felt very discouraged. Ty knelt down by my feet, looking up into my face.

"What's wrong?" he asked.

"Having cancer isn't very much fun," I replied.

He continued to talk to me quietly, making jokes to lighten the mood. I rallied myself (after all, I had a room full of guests), and was able to be in better spirits. A little later, as I replayed the fiasco in my head, I felt so impressed, and quite happy, at Ty's presence of mind. A lot of people can't handle the sight of blood, and understandably so. But once again, the Lord showed me the specialness of my situation. He showed me, not for the first time, the great blessing he gave me in having such a reliable man. After all, how many girls have their blood spewing from their IV and are then rescued by their knight in shining armor? I don't know of anyone else. So the Lord gave me something to be very thankful for from my IV explosion.

Alice Adjustments

Her hair is given her for a covering. (1 Corinthians 11:15b)

As I mentioned previously, I was really upset about the idea of losing my hair. But the Lord let me keep it longer than expected. And, thankfully, he made me with really thick hair, so that even after losing three-quarters of it (my hair was almost shoulder length then), I still had hair all over my entire head. Since my hair was now so thin, though, it began looking a little sad and straggly.

But from being a stylist, I knew that if people with thin hair cut it shorter, the hair instantly appears thicker. Thus, I desperately needed a haircut. I worked at the Penton House Salon and Day Spa (a great place to get your hair and spa services done if you're near Pace, Florida!) up until the day I left for urgent care (and then the hospital), and found out I had cancer. So happily, I knew just where to go for my much-needed hair adjustment.

My boss, Alice (who is very dear to me and has since claimed me as the daughter she never had because of our similar features and personalities), came to my rescue. She, praise the Lord, is the type of person who will do anything for anyone who needs help. And I needed help! I called her and asked if she would please cut my hair, assuming it would stay on my head long enough. She eagerly agreed, and so off I went to give my degraded state of hair a pick-me-up. Oh, faithful Alice. The girls at the salon told me that before I arrived, she had all of them scouring the entire salon, making sure my almost extinct immune system wouldn't be compromised. No germ, dirt, or speck of dust could possibly escape its swift and sure destruction.

So in I walked (Ty accompanying me), marveling at how drastically my life and circumstances had changed in just a matter of weeks. My station sat empty, void of any trace of my former presence. My Energizer-Bunny, won't-sit-down part of my personality had, for now at least, ceased. Already I felt tired from the exertion of walking from the car, to the salon, to Alice's chair. Praise the Lord, I didn't feel dejected about this change—just more aware of how drastic it was. I gingerly sat in Alice's chair, staring at my reduced hair density. My somewhat see-through hair strands clung resolutely to my scalp, sparing me from eventual but inevitable baldness.

Once we discussed what she would do, we walked to the shampoo-bowl room where I enjoyed a marvelous hair wash and head massage. As I sat in the chair, though, I could feel more hair slipping from my head. Although Alice got very quiet, she didn't lose her composure with me, which I appreciated. (I'd worked for her and her husband, Doug, for four years, and we had a close relationship.) Alice finished with my shampoo and conditioner and, keeping a cheerful countenance, brought me back to her station.

As she gently combed out my hair, yet more strands became deserters. I started getting worried. I didn't want to lose so much that I'd be forced to shave my head! I wasn't ready for that yet! But the Lord kindly and mercifully commanded what was left of my diminished, now definitely see-through hair, to stay put.

I felt slightly demoralized about my wispy hair, but the Lord had the situation more than under control. As Alice cut off a couple of inches, putting my hair at chin length, it stopped looking so forlorn and destitute. My thin little hair perked right up, and I immediately felt encouraged by my makeover. Even my face didn't look so thin and drawn. The Lord, who knows the end from the beginning, put me in a salon years before my cancer with a loving boss and friend, who he used as a comfort and great help in my time of need. My Alice Adjustments to my hair, as I have since affectionately nicknamed it, turned out to be a very dear blessing from the Lord.

That evening, in fact, to celebrate my new hairdo, Tyler took me out for dinner. I couldn't last very long, but Laura took pictures of our special date. It was one of the last times I was able to go out to a restaurant for a long time, and one of the last times I had enough hair to go out without a scarf. The Lord was so good to allow me to have that special night. A night where I still had my hair as my covering. A night where I weakly but contentedly sat beside the man I loved for a final meal out. And, especially, a night where my Alice Adjustments made all the difference.

18

Picture Perfect

Bear ye one another's burdens, and so fulfil
the law of Christ. (Galatians 6:2)

In my opinion, my pastor was one of the best pastors to have ever walked the face of the earth. (Not that I'm biased or anything!) This is some of my reasoning: he was the epitome of a faithful man. The Bible says, "But a faithful man who can find?" (Proverbs 20:6b). He was faithful to the Lord. If any man ever "prayed without ceasing" (1 Thessalonians 5:17), it was him. He faithfully read his Bible. In fact, by the time he died, he'd read through it well over four hundred times. He told others about Jesus Christ everywhere he went. I tell you all these details about him, my dear reader, because the Lord used him to have a very major influence on my life. He *lived* what he believed. I sat under him starting at eleven years old, and never once saw an ounce of hypocrisy in his life. He was real with his congregation. He preached the truth using the Bible as his final authority—not his own opinions, philosophies, or other popular beliefs. Although he preached hard, not sugar-coating difficult topics, I also saw a side of him that revealed a man of true compassion. I saw him shed tears over Christians who were hurting, as well as tears over lost souls. He faithfully ministered to people behind the scenes.

I want to tell you an act of love and kindness he did for me that served as a great source of comfort and encouragement throughout my cancer.

My pastor, Dr. Ruckman, was a talented artist. When he preached on Sunday night, he drew a chalk picture to illustrate the sermon. When he found out I had cancer, he picked up his oil paints (which he hadn't touched in three years because of his failing eyesight), and painted a picture for me. He painted a picture of a girl (me) lying in a hospital bed. You can tell she's very sick. Standing halfway behind the bed is a picture of Jesus standing over her. He has on a crown of thorns, and one of his hands is resting on the back of the bedframe while the other is stretched around the bed, holding the girl's hand in his own. You can see the nail prints in his hands. His crown of thorns and nail prints are a reminder that Jesus is "a man of sorrows, and acquainted with grief" (Isaiah 53:3b), and that he knows what it is to suffer (Hebrews 12:2–3). To the left of the bed, hanging on the wall, is a clock with the time reading just before eleven o'clock, or what is known as "the eleventh hour." The eleventh hour represents when a trial is almost over. In my case, when my trial of having cancer is almost done—almost over. It was a precious reminder that I wasn't going through this time alone and that this trial wasn't going to last forever. Jesus Christ was with me every step of the way. He promised he'd "never leave me nor forsake me" (Hebrews 13:5c).

I cannot express to you the overwhelming comfort that picture gave me. It hung on the wall next to the clock in my room (ironically) where it was in plain sight at all times.

When Laura came home one day, all smiles, with a surprise for me from our pastor, I remember opening the package and just staring at the picture. As a general rule, my pastor didn't actually paint pictures for people (although he always gave away his Sunday night "chalk talk" picture) because when you have a congregation of over five hundred people, you typically can't paint just one person a picture.

Yet here I sat, on my bed, in my newly broken-in room (I had lived with Laura for about a month by then), holding this precious treasure in my hands. I waited until Laura left the room, and then I just wept. I felt so touched and grateful. What a reminder of Jesus Christ's compassion—of his constant presence during our darkest hours. And what an act of love and compassion from my pastor! He painted a picture that fit and ministered to my specific situation so perfectly. I was so blessed to have him as my pastor.

Dr. Ruckman was ninety-one years old when he painted that picture for me. The Lord took him home a few years later, at age ninety-four. My oil painting was the last one he ever did. I felt and feel so humbled and honored to have received that priceless painting. Words can't express how much it meant, and still means to me to this day. And that, my dear reader, is one of God's special, tender blessings and mercies that only comes from going through a very hard trial. In my case, stage four cancer—a time that had plenty of hardship and suffering, but also a time of many precious blessings I wouldn't have received any other way.

19

Refreshed By Mrs. Ruckman

The Lord give mercy unto the house of Onesiphorus;
for he oft refreshed me. (2 Timothy 1:16a)

I've seen a prayer request section on church bulletins that names the shut-ins of the congregation. Shut-ins are those who are either too ill or physically unable to leave the house. I never realized how much prayer a shut-in needed until I temporarily became one.

But the Lord is so kind. He never gave me more than I could bear, and faithfully sent help and comfort to me when I needed it most. My pastor's wife, Mrs. Ruckman, came over to visit me. She really had a heart to minister, and ministered to me more that day she came over than she'll ever know. I've known her since I was eleven years old, and as my pastor's wife, I've watched her faithful example of a godly woman. I also listened to her sound counsel over the years. To give you some background, she used to watch us young church kids for three hours on Wednesday night while our parents attended Bible classes. Every week, she faithfully emphasized missions and our missionaries' various foreign fields. I still remember her holding up flash cards of the flags of foreign countries. She'd ask who could name the country as well as the missionary stationed there. Occasionally, if a missionary passed through on a furlough (a brief break from the field), she'd have them come in and talk to us kids about their country. I mention this because the Bible says, "Train up a child in the way he should go: and when he is old, he will not depart from it" (Proverbs 22:6). She, along with her husband and my pastor, Dr. Ruckman, really instilled in me an awareness and burden for missions. This added fuel to my already strong desire to be a missionary. But, that comes into play in another section.

Then, years later, during my shut-in status, she continued her trend of being a blessing in many different ways. But the one that stands out the most was when she came over to Laura's to visit me. She brought along a detoxing foot bath, a potted flower plant, and a card. We visited for a few hours, and I really enjoyed the time. She showed me how to use the foot bath and provided me with very uplifting company and fellowship. We not only chatted about trivial subjects but also on a heart-to-heart level. The Lord really does bring help to his children and refreshes them in his perfect timing. And this particular time, he orchestrated me to be refreshed by Mrs. Ruckman.

20
Blood Transfusions

But my God shall supply all your need. (Philippians 4:19a)

I didn't want a blood transfusion. The thought of having some stranger's blood, which may or may not have some terrible disease, terrified me. But I was becoming increasingly weaker, and my blood cell counts remained very low. Thank God my numbers never plummeted into the critical stage, but they kept coming very close.

My doctor suggested a blood transfusion a couple of different times, explaining that it would really help me feel better and get stronger. Furthermore, it would give my body a much-needed boost to fight the cancer. But I couldn't bring myself to take the risk, although slight, of receiving tainted blood. Ah, but my loving Lord and Savior poured out his tender mercies once again. He already had all the details worked out and graciously provided me with yet another amazing blessing.

I think it was Laura who told me that there's such a thing as direct donation. Individuals that I knew could donate their blood specifically to me. Now that changed everything, and thank God it did! I ended up having not just one, but three blood transfusions during the course of my cancer.

Each blood transfusion involved a long process (at least for me). First, the nurses at the infusion center prepped me with Benadryl and some other medications. They also hooked me up to a heart monitor to make sure my body was receiving—and not rejecting—the new blood. We always waited a long time for the blood to be brought up from the lab (where it had been stored) to the infusion center. Then, with Tyler beside me in the large recliner chair, and our trusty DVD player ready to go, the nurses attached my transfusion bag (through a tube) to my port.

My port was a device that had been surgically implanted into the right side of my chest before I started my chemotherapy treatments. The port provided a way to take or receive blood and administer fluids, chemo, and medications intravenously without having to continually stick a needle in my veins. My port was a godsend, because anytime I needed labs taken, the nurses inserted a needle into the port, drawing blood from my heart's blood supply. This proved to be super helpful because eventually I became so weak, the veins in my arms stopped giving blood when a nurse stuck them with a needle. So you can see, with my blood volume that low, I really needed these blood transfusions.

I felt so touched by those who donated for me! Six people who I love very dearly donated their blood—without my even asking! Laura and her whole family, which included her dad and my associate pastor, Brother Donovan, Mrs. Donovan, and Emily, along with Brother and Mrs. Turner, all selflessly donated their blood to help me fight cancer—to help save my life. My gratitude and love for them is beyond description. Let me give you a brief background on all of them. Laura and Mrs. Donovan both have low blood sugar. They knew that when they donated their blood, they would both feel (and did feel) really ill the rest of that day. Poor Laura could barely get off the couch after she got home because she felt so weak.

I already had a close relationship with Mrs. Donovan before I got cancer. Along with being my associate pastor's wife, she was my Sunday school teacher throughout junior high. I remember one time during class, she told all of us girls, "Start praying now for the Lord to give you a good husband. There aren't many good guys left, but the Lord can save one for you." I started praying for the Lord to do just that from then on. I was twelve or thirteen and in seventh grade. Boy, did the Lord use that small but invaluable bit of advice! I prayed, and the Lord did "exceeding abundantly above all that I asked or thought" (Ephesians 3:20a), as I'm sure you've been able to see through some of these stories. Mrs. Donovan also talked and counselled with me over the years, helping me through some hard times, and also just took time to chat with me. She always told me she was praying for me, and that meant the world to me. She sat and visited with me numerous times throughout the course of my cancer. Her help and encouragement during my storm ministered to me so deeply. The Lord really used her in my life, and still uses her to this day.

As for Brother Donovan, who could ask for a more a wonderful, devoted pastor? He took time out of his busy schedule to donate blood for me. I've seen through the years how much he ministers to his members behind the scenes. The Lord had also used his preaching, teaching, and time with us kids when I was in the youth group to really help me grow in the Lord and get a closer relationship with Jesus Christ. And that kind of blessing influenced my entire life—not to mention that it has eternal value. He taught several Bible classes in our church's Bible institute, and the Lord used them to help me grow as well. These classes gave me such a deeper love and knowledge of the Bible and of the Lord's character. I loved all of them tremendously. He's always been such an outstanding example to me. He also visited me when I was in the hospital and came over to Laura's with Mrs. Donovan for visits too. These visits meant everything to me—the Lord used them to help me in a very special way.

I'd known Emily, Laura's younger sister and the Donovans' other daughter, for years (I think since she was about five years old). I helped tutor her in math for a short time. She was always sweet, kind, and friendly. By the time I needed blood donations, I knew she was really busy with work and didn't have a ton of time on her hands. Regarding her personality, she tends to be more quiet and reserved until you get to know her. (Of course, when she opens up, she's not only really great to talk to, but also very intuitive.) So my initially quiet friend Em, without making any type of proclamation, silently decided to be one of my donors.

I'd known Brother and Mrs. Turner since I was eleven years old (same as the Donovans). Their sons and I were in the youth group together. Sometimes Mrs. Turner substitute taught the high school Sunday school class, and did a great job. I always looked forward to her lessons. She also came on youth group activities and was a ton of fun. Brother Turner taught (and still teaches) visitation (soul-winning) and theology in our church's Bible institute. I loved his classes. He always cracked me up with his dry and sarcastic sense of humor. He also showed so much concern and compassion for lost souls as well as a desire to minister to hurting Christians. I remember him saying in class one time that the Lord's call for him was to "be a help" (from 1 Corinthians 12:28), however and wherever possible. And he does just that. He came and visited me (along with Brother Dunson) in the hospital after my worst night of cancer. I remember slowly turning my head in my hospital bed when they came in, and I will never forget how kind he was and how much I appreciated having him and Brother Dunson there.

So these were the people the Lord provided for me to be able to get direct donation blood transfusions. Without them, I don't know how much harder of a time I would've had with the cancer, or if I even would've made it. The Lord is so faithful, dear reader. He showed me that no one else can orchestrate circumstances like he can. He showed me that I'm never helpless—I always have him to go to, and that the verse is absolutely true that promises, "But my God shall supply all your need according to his riches in glory by Christ Jesus" (Philippians 4:19).

Years later, when the Lord miraculously allowed me to get pregnant and give birth to our wonderful son David (and now we have another son on the way!), Tyler and I insisted that Brother and Mrs. Donovan be one of the sets of his grandparents, and Brother and Mrs. Turner too. Laura and Emily are his aunts. After all, I have both Turner and Donovan blood running through my veins—and I'm very honored to have it!

21

Life-Saving Counsel

How forcible are right words. (Job 6:25a)

I cannot fully convey to you, my dear reader, the extent of how weak I had become toward the end of my chemo treatments. Thank God the Lord gave me a lot of grace, because by this time, I had been almost completely bedridden for months. I lacked the physical ability to run, jump, skip, or hop. I knew this for a fact because one time, when Ty came over to Laura's after work, I felt so ecstatic to see him I attempted a slight skip to get to him faster. My atrophied legs buckled, and I almost crashed to the ground. The realization of my weakened state was a hard blow for me. Even when I walked, I could only shuffle to and fro.

On top of all this, I reached a very scary point: I literally, legitimately thought I was going insane. I began to have terrible episodes. I felt like I was on fire just beneath the surface of my skin. Sometimes I would break out in a cold sweat and feel trapped inside my body. I banged my head against my pillow (scaring Tyler to death and horrifying him too) because I felt so restless and like I was losing my mind. Although I had no desire to kill myself, I randomly started having suicidal thoughts. These few days proved to be some of the scariest I experienced during cancer. I thought these horrific meltdowns resulted from my chemotherapy drugs. I told Tyler, "I would rather die sane than live insane. I think the chemo is starting to make me go crazy."

One of the last days of this, when I was having a particularly rough time, Tyler reached a breaking point. He watched as I writhed in pain, broken out in a cold sweat, beating my head against my pillow. I told him, over and over, "I feel so sick and so strange. I don't know what to do! My skin is on fire! It feels like bugs are crawling underneath the surface of my skin. I'm trapped inside my body!" Ty prayed for me like crazy and tried to calm me down the best he could. Holding back tears, he encouraged me to try to get some sleep. And, by a miracle of God, I finally did fall asleep. Once Ty could tell I was sleeping soundly, he went into the living room and fell to his knees before the Lord. He begged and cried for the Lord to make me better and take away this nightmare of a situation. He told the Lord he was at the end of his rope and couldn't handle this. He "poured out his complaint" (1 Samuel 1:15–16) before the Lord, feeling sheer desperation.

After a long time spent pleading at the Lord's throne of grace (Hebrews 4:16), he got up and came back into my room. Within minutes, I woke up, looked him in the eyes with my now clear, non-glossed-over-from-pain-and-agony eyes, and said simply, "I feel better." He just sat on the side of my bed and wept, praising and thanking the Lord. He later told me that that was a turning point for him in his relationship with the Lord. He saw God's faithfulness in such a special way, and experienced his supernatural grace. When he felt he physically and emotionally had reached his breaking point, and that he had been drained of the last bit of strength and fortitude to deal with this situation, he saw the Lord step in. He saw the Lord intervene, and he lived the truth of the verse that says, "I can do all things through Christ which strengtheneth me" (Philippians 4:13). The Lord gave him just the right amount of strength and help he needed, when he needed it.

Although I felt better for several hours, by that night my

condition took another downward spiral. These fits came back. Determined to get me off the chemo, Tyler made an appointment for me with Dr. Collins. We felt sure the Lord must be showing us we should stop treatments and do natural methods instead.

My dad ended up being the one to come to my appointment (Ty had to work that day). I sat on the exam table and described my symptoms to Dr. Collins. I told her I felt the chemo was causing me to go insane and that I had to stop having it. She asked me a few more questions, shocking me by pinpointing some other smaller details that went with these episodes, which I hadn't told her. She explained to me that what I experienced wasn't from the chemotherapy treatments. "You're having withdrawals from your pain medication," she explained. During my visit, she asked me how frequently I was taking my new pain medication. (I had been on morphine, a twelve-hour, slow-release dose that I took twice a day. She wanted to get me off the morphine, and switched me to a different painkiller that I had to take every four to six hours, or as needed. Miraculously, I wasn't in constant pain, so I didn't take the medication as often as I could have.) When I told her how frequently (or rather, how infrequently) I took this new pain medication, she said that my body was used to having pain medication (a narcotic) in my system for twenty-four hours of the day. Now that that timeframe had suddenly and significantly lessened, my body was going through withdrawals. The remedy: take my new pain medication more often at first, then slowly start cutting it back. Soon I would only have to take it as often as my pain dictated.

I sat in that little office room completely confused and miserable. I had felt sure the Lord wanted me to come off the chemo, using these horrific side effects from it as a sign. But now, I realized the chemo wasn't the culprit of my insanity. And frankly, the thought of having to be super disciplined and rigid about diet, supplements, etc. (if I did alternative medicine) scared me to death. But I didn't want to have to endure any more chemo! I felt so weary from being sick. By now I weighed seventy-eight pounds (pretty much skin and bones) and was basically completely bald. I felt very discouraged and despondent. All I wanted was to feel better and be better! As I said earlier, I had become very weak and just passed day after day lying in bed with no energy or ability to get out. I was sick of this seemingly wasted existence, having nothing but a pathetic excuse of a life.

I remember sitting there, completely conflicted, and as my lips began to tremble, I locked my arms around my knees, with my feet resting on the table. I buried my face in my knees and just cried. I told Dr. Collins, "I just don't want to do chemo anymore! I *can't* do it anymore—I can't take it anymore! I don't have the strength for it!"

She came over to me, hugged me, and gently reminded me, "But when you can't, that's when *he* (God) can." I slowly nodded my head. She prayed with me and encouraged me to continue the chemo. I called Ty on the way back home and told him what she had said. He stayed quiet for a few seconds and then replied, "Well, we'll just pray about it."

He had already gotten advice from several people, all of whom told him to take me off the chemo. Even after he told the new information to a couple of people, they still counseled him to get me off the chemo (understandably so) since it was so hard on my body. But, Ty still felt unsettled about the decision, so he prayed hard and went to talk to our associate pastor, Brother Donovan.

Tyler gave him all the details of what I'd been experiencing, what the doctor had said, and added that several people were encouraging him to take me off the chemo. But praise the Lord for Brother Donovan! I honestly believe the Lord used his counsel, as well as Dr. Collins's counsel, to save my life. Brother Donovan suggested, "If the chemo is *working*, keep her on it. If she can stand to take more treatments—even if she can barely stand it—if she can stand it at all, *make her take it*." Tyler told him he'd pray about it and left his office to further seek the Lord. He told me later that he was all set to have me stop the chemo until he talked with Brother Donovan. He said he didn't like what he heard because he knew how hard of a time I was having. But by the time he got back to Laura's, both he and I, from praying separately, felt sure the Lord wanted me to continue the chemo. The chemo was working and had already greatly reduced the amount of cancer in my body. We both had perfect peace about the decision.

And you know what, my dear reader? That next treatment of chemo I took after this abhorrent experience turned out to be the last one I needed. What a merciful God! I wanted to quit after my fifth treatment. I literally believed I had reached my breaking point and couldn't possibly take anymore. Oh, but God, in his wisdom, knew that I just needed to endure one more aggressive treatment—just one, and then the cancer was gone. My scan came back 100 percent clear! I took my medication more frequently, and my body behaved.

To this day, I am sure the Lord used Dr. Collins's counsel to help save my life. The Lord gave her wisdom to know the cause of my distress and how to fix it. If we had just stopped the chemo and not talked to Dr. Collins, the problem would've still existed. I would've stayed in a really bad way, not knowing what to do to help it.

And although Ty and I trusted Dr. Collins, we both not only trusted Brother Donovan—but also knew him—for much longer. I'd grown up in my church in Florida since I was eleven years old. I knew Brother Donovan cared about me and hated to see me suffering, but I also knew he had a close relationship with the Lord and a lot of spiritual discernment. I know the Lord gave him the wisdom to give tough advice: to have Tyler make me keep doing something that caused me to be miserable at times but was for my good. Something that, in the long run, would save my life.

The Lord used Brother Donovan's advice as the push Ty needed to have me endure my awful chemotherapy. And, again, the Lord used that last chemotherapy session to completely clear any remaining cancer. He also showed me how important seeking him in prayer is for every decision. He is so faithful! I'm so thankful for his continual protection and provision! And, in this case, his provision was through invaluable, lifesaving counsel.

My Mom's Spaghetti

And having food and raiment let us be
therewith content. (1 Timothy 6:8)

I love spaghetti! Italian food, namely pasta (and pizza too), is my favorite kind of food. As I mentioned previously, I couldn't eat many different foods during cancer. My chemo drastically affected my appetite and taste buds. I realized early on that if I got a specific craving, I needed to act on it quickly. If I waited too long to have that food, my desire for it went away, and I ended up not eating anything.

One particular food I craved frequently was spaghetti. Laura faithfully cooked whatever I wanted like a real trooper, and she made phenomenal spaghetti. She's Italian, so needless to say, she made (and still makes) a smashing marinara sauce, along with noodles cooked to perfection.

But I remember one time in particular when I was in the hospital, I specifically wanted my mom's spaghetti. No other spaghetti would do. She, like Laura, made her sauce from scratch (with no meat because I prefer my sauce plain), and it always tasted delicious to me, as well as comforting and familiar. So I called her and asked her to please make her spaghetti and bring it to me. And, oh, when she arrived with it and I filled my palette with its scrumptious goodness, pure happiness erupted in my mouth. My taste buds were thrilled, I was happy; and, after polishing off that pasta, my stomach was full.

There were other times too when, all of a sudden, all I wanted was my mom's spaghetti. And when she came over with it, I always merrily stuffed myself as much as I was able. Thank God for that pasta pick-me-up! After all, sometimes, when you're sick, you just need good, old-fashioned comfort food. And for me, that meant one thing: my mom's spaghetti.

23

Beauty School Dropout

Support the weak. (1 Thessalonians 5:14c)

I had several professors in college who I really enjoyed, but Dr. Miklovich, or Dr. Mik, was my favorite. He was in his sixties, with white hair combed to the side and a neatly trimmed white beard. He lectured and moved about with gusto, which fit his assertive yet fun personality. His knowledge of European history, specializing in the United Kingdom, was unbelievable. To me, he represented a never-ending encyclopedia of information. He received his PhD from Cambridge University, so his experiences living in England for a period of years really enhanced his grasp of its history and culture. His classes were always comprehensive and fascinating. I loved his dry sense of humor and sarcastic wisecracks—he left me giggling so often that I sometimes struggled with taking the copious notes required to do well in his classes. I loved his teaching and really appreciated him as a person too.

My friend Kayla and I took as many of his classes as we could. Poor Dr. Mik wouldn't have been able to get rid of us if he'd tried. Being veterans of his classes gave us a glorious opportunity, which I'm still so pleased about I must share the story with you. It was the opportunity to pull a prank! One time (probably the only time Dr. Mik was ever late for class), on the day our research papers were due, Kayla and I convinced our entire class (with the exception of a few nervous souls) to set all the research papers in a stack on his desk and leave the room. We all hid just outside the building, thrilled with our bravery and brilliance. Dr. Miklovich *hated* it when a student came late to class, so this was only fair! Our tardy professor came into an almost empty classroom, the only evidence of our former presence being the research papers and few sticks-in-the-muds who divulged our plan to him. He tromped outside to find his guilty but pleased-as-punch students all huddled together, grinning broadly. He instantly assessed the culprits (Kayla and I) and, with mock seriousness, told us to beg for mercy. We, of course, only smiled more brightly. All of us filed back to class and, everyone being in a good humor (after us guilty ones had glared slightly at the obedient ones), enjoyed a great class.

Dr. Mik nicknamed me "beauty school dropout" (he told me he stole that label from the movie *Grease)* because I worked in a salon as a hairstylist all throughout college. He always looked so proud of himself when he called me that because of the irony of the joke. (I remained a hopeless perfectionist throughout all my classes, and, during his classes especially, I wrote furiously, not wanting to miss a single detail. After all, I wanted to learn as much as I could and loathed anything lower than an A.). So, at the beginning of a semester, at the first class of the semester, he called roll, merrily referring to me as "beauty school dropout."

When he found out I had cancer, my wonderful former professor came to Laura's to visit me. I felt very touched over his concern. He brought me two potted plants: one of yellow flowers, and the other of a fern for my garden for when I got well. He visited for a while, sitting next to my bed, and we merrily talked and joked. I listened to him tell me stories of his traveling adventures. (Dr. Mik not only traveled all over the world, but was a master storyteller). We had a wonderful time. At one point, I remember he held my hand and told me, "You're going to get well. You're going to pull through this."

I felt so encouraged from his visit. Being cut off from almost all social life was very hard for me, so the Lord, in his goodness, brought some of society to me. My small room, which proved the sole of my existence during cancer, occasionally came alive with laughter, stories, and precious memories that will last forever. I'm so thankful to the Lord for my visitors. I never realized what a long way one visit can go to help break the feeling of extreme seclusion and loneliness.

And as for Dr. Mik, I still remember his reaction when I called to tell him my cancer was gone. He was elated! He later told me that he stayed in a daze for the rest of that day. When his wife, Libby, came home and saw his expression, she asked what had happened. He replied, "It's Katy."

She sadly responded, "She didn't make it?"

"No," he clarified with awe. "She's better!"

Dr. Mik and his wife came to our wedding, and he even got to meet our little son, David, about a year after he was born. (We had moved to Colorado and were back in Florida for a visit.)

I always loved Dr. Mik, but his visit during my cancer solidified him as even more meaningful to me. I really appreciated the Lord's faithfulness in giving me just the encouragement I needed at a discouraging time: a visit from my history college professor to his little beauty school dropout. And that visit now remains a very treasured part of *my* history.

24

The Adventures of Smog and Fritz

Edify one another. (1 Thessalonians 5:11b)

Ty is a spectacular storyteller. Starting from his young teenage years and continuing into adulthood, he created fascinating stories. I remember times during Bible school when, at a get-together, he'd tell some of his stories to a group of us students. Our attention remained riveted on him. The Lord gifted him with such an incredible imagination, as well as the ability to come up with these well-composed, interesting, exhilarating, and suspenseful stories (need I add more adjectives to make my point?).

One thing I've noticed over and over again with the Lord is how many different ways he will use a talent. For example, Ty told his already formulated stories to many eager listeners. He also regularly came up with new stories that he texted to his cousin in Tennessee. Beginning from when we first started talking, Ty visited me at work. We sat together on the front porch and, as we watched the ever-present squirrels scampering around the lawn of the salon, he invented random, hilarious stories about them too.

Then cancer came. My hour upon hour of vegetating in bed left me feeling discouraged and restless, more than I like to remember. But the Lord, knowing the end from the beginning—including every detail of life—hand-picked Tyler just for me. He gave me someone who kept me both encouraged and entertained with his vast imagination and God-given storytelling ability. Thus, it was during my bout with cancer that *The Adventures of Smog and Fritz* materialized. One day, while lying in my bed feeling pretty discouraged, I asked Ty to please tell me a story—to make one up just for me. Without missing a beat, Tyler began, "Once upon a time, there was a dog named Smog. He lived with his beloved but geeky owner Casey ..." Ty then launched into this entire story about Smog, Casey, and Fritz. Fritz was Casey's cat and Smog's eternal antagonist. Fritz always attempted to out-wit Smog and get him into some kind of trouble or funny predicament. Fritz strategically planned his antagonizing when Casey's girlfriend, Valentine, came over to visit or when Casey had to leave to run an errand.

During many of the adventures of Smog and Fritz, Fritz, the sly and snooty cat, victoriously bested poor Smog (as these were short, oral stories that soon became a regular series, fashioned similarly to a comic strip anecdote like *Garfield* or *Marmaduke*). But occasionally, Smog triumphed over Fritz's attempted trouble, and I inwardly cheered over the happy-go-lucky dog's success.

So these fun, humorous, and quirky stories, which I loved immensely and begged for frequently, became a much-needed bright spot during some of my dismal days. What a precious Lord I have and serve, who gave me someone with such a splendid talent—a talent that he knew would cheer me up time and time again. My own adventure with cancer was enhanced by the adventures of a certain dog and cat—the adventures of Smog and Fritz.

25

A Mountain Proposal

O magnify the LORD with me, and let us
exalt his name together. (Psalm 34:3)

About one week before Christmas, I went in for a CT scan
to see how much cancer, if any, remained. By this time, I
had had a total of six chemotherapy treatments (one every
three weeks) and two lumbar punctures. I didn't want to know
the results of the scan until after Christmas. After all, I was about
to go on vacation and wanted all thoughts of chemo and tests out
of my mind. Laura and Peter already informed me a month earlier
that they'd be out of town for two weeks at Christmastime. So Ty
whisked me off to his home state of Colorado for a week to spend
time with his family and celebrate Christmas together.

We endured a horrendous plane ride—I remained very ill
the whole day, and Ty had to cart me around the airport in a
wheelchair throughout this whole excursion (which included
before our first flight, in between our second connection, and
after, since I was too weak and sick to walk much). But Colorado
proved to be beautiful. His family lived in Divide, which is forty-
five minutes outside of Colorado Springs, in the mountains. We
could actually see Pike's Peak from town. I loved the prairie feel of

Divide—the wheat-colored vegetation mixed with the mountains and snow showcased a beauty I had never seen before.

I felt so blessed to be able to get out of town and travel to my Ty's stomping-grounds. His grandparents arrived a few days before us, so I got to meet them too. Although I remained pretty ill during our visit, Ty and I were able to go into town together one day. I had my purple headscarf over my absent hair, my very loose-fitting long, denim skirt (that poor skirt hung on me, I'm sad to say, as a result of all the weight I'd lost), a navy blue hoodie, very little makeup, and brown snow boots. Thus we set out, with me in my sad mountain attire, and Tyler, who always looked tremendous, in his jeans, boots, and button-up black shirt.

We ran an errand first and then ate at a tasty local Chinese restaurant. We also stopped at his dad's work so Ty could get the keys to show me his dad's church. His dad had started and pastored a small church in Divide beginning from when Tyler was fourteen years old. I could tell Ty was really excited to show it to me. We walked inside, and I enjoyed exploring the building. We headed up to the podium to check out the stage, and Ty said, "You know, I get so excited thinking about this place. I think of how one day the Lord might call us up here to Colorado to help with my dad's church. I'd be up here preaching while you sit supportively in the front row." He paused, looked at me, smiled, and interjected, "Go ahead and sit in the front row." I obediently and happily took my seat.

"I think of my preaching up here," he continued, "and looking down at you," (again another smile) "and maybe a few other little Campbells." Now there was a broader smile from him at the thought of us having children, despite what I was told. "And how great it would be to serve the Lord together." He walked down the steps and sat down next to me. "I think about us having fun together, and about us going to the altar and praying together, and just living our lives together. There's one verse in the Bible that always makes me think of us. It says, 'O magnify the LORD with me, and let us exalt his name together.' So I guess what I'm wondering is ..." He then pulled out a ring and knelt down on one knee. "Will you magnify the Lord with me and let us exalt his name together? Katy, will you marry me?"

I don't know if my smile had ever been bigger.

"Of course!" I exclaimed, trembling with happiness and excitement.

He slipped the ring onto my finger, and I flung my tiny self at him in as big of a hug as I could muster. He looked back up at me (he was still on one knee) and said, "Does that mean yes?" (I think he just wanted to hear that magic three-letter word.)

"Yes!" I laughingly and excitedly proclaimed. Then I gave him another huge hug.

I remember tears streaming down my face as I looked back and forth from my handsome fiancé to my beautiful ring during the car ride back. I felt so grateful and fulfilled and loved. I was going to marry this amazing man of my prayers and dreams! My cup overflowed.

Ty proposed on December 21, 2011. Nine days later, on December 30, 2011, we found out my cancer was gone. The scan had come back completely clear. Although I still had to do maintenance chemo for one year, we knew the Lord had spared my life. And I couldn't wait to use my life to try to live out that precious verse: to magnify the Lord with Tyler and exalt God's name together.

26

Wedding Wonder

This is my beloved, and this is my
friend. (Song of Solomon 5:16b)

Tyler and I were married on June 2, 2012. I couldn't have
asked for a more perfect wedding. Brother Donovan
performed our ceremony. He quoted Ephesians 2:4a "But
God, who is rich in mercy." He talked about a time, several months
ago, when he took a long walk down a hospital corridor, expecting
to be meeting for a funeral about this time of year. "But God …"
Instead we were all meeting here for a wedding.

I am so humbled that the Lord chose to spare my life. He truly
"made everything beautiful in his time" (Ecclesiastes 3:11a). The
joy of having what felt like the crumbled walls of my life rebuilt
through God's mercy is indescribable. I feel that the Lord truly
gave me "beauty for ashes" (Isaiah 61:3b). What a precious gift,
and what a transformation!

I remember having such deep peace and contentment the day
of my wedding—and, of course, happiness beyond belief. It was
a dream come true. Friends, family, and relatives attended from
all over the country. Approximately 350 people celebrated this
miraculous day with us. Laura, along with my other best friend,
Hannah, stood as my matrons of honor. Four other dear friends

of mine were my bridesmaids. My girls were all decked out in different colored dresses. Laura and Hannah wore blue while my other girls filed down the aisle in green, purple, yellow, and coral.

The Lord provided for every detail so graciously. His provisions were so overwhelming, in fact, that I must list them to you, dear reader—they were that special to us, and it's a testimony of how the Lord can be trusted for both big and little things. Before the wedding, I obviously hadn't been able to work, and Ty had taken off a great deal of time to help with my care. We therefore had very little money for the wedding. But the Lord once again did "exceeding abundantly above all that we could ask or think" (Ephesians 3:20). Alice had a friend named Howard who had heard about my story and gave me all of my flower arrangements, boutonnieres, and bouquets for only one hundred dollars! What a blessing!

My cousin Leah made a delicious Superman groom's cake for our reception. It looked like it was from a magazine, and tasted just as good! She also explained our situation to her mother-in-law, who just so happened to still have a warehouse full of wedding decorations (she used to own her own wedding shop). Her mother-in-law graciously and generously allowed us to use whatever we wanted, free of charge. So we were blessed with a beautiful candelabrum, candle fixtures along the aisle, small pillars, a table for our unity sand, and other detail pieces that added wonderful finishing touches. Alice talked to her pastor, who allowed us to use their church fellowship hall (my church's building was too small) for our reception free of charge! Alice and other of my coworkers decorated the entire building, and it looked absolutely beautiful.

Doug and Alice gave us their timeshare to use for our honeymoon, thus providing us with a free and incredible resort in Montana (five days, four nights). Peter's niece Emileigh photographed our wedding and reception. The pictures turned out gorgeous, and she only charged us $250. My friend Melanie made a stunning wedding cake for us as a wedding gift. Our guests raved about how delicious it tasted, and I fully agreed! Alice styled my hair, of course, and I couldn't have been more thrilled with the results. (Tyler was thrilled too!)

The Lord's hand guided and provided for all the details that went into the wedding preparations. He also provided money for me to purchase the "dress of my dreams," as I have since referred to it. And, because I'm a female, I must devote a couple of paragraphs telling you the story about my gown.

Laura practically dragged me out of bed to pick out my wedding dress. I still lived almost solely in bed, as my body struggled to recover from the rigors of cancer and chemotherapy ... not to mention that I was still taking maintenance chemo. Laura kept tactfully insisting that I needed to go dress shopping soon or else they wouldn't be able to order the dress in time for the wedding. I consistently turned her down, moaning that I didn't feel well enough. (And I did feel miserable—you know a girl is sick if she's not up to going wedding dress shopping!) Finally one day, she entered my room and kindly but firmly informed me that she scheduled an appointment for me with David's Bridal. Thank God for Laura! I really don't think I would've gotten my wedding dress in time if it hadn't been for her—I really needed a push to get out of bed!

So I went to David's Bridal, accompanied by Laura, Dana, and Lydia. At first I took my scarf off my head—after all, I was trying on wedding gowns and wanted to see it without my scarf on! But after nearly bursting into tears over my devastating appearance (several dresses just didn't do anything for my tiny frame, and having buzz-cut length hair certainly didn't help the situation), I meekly returned my scarf to its dutiful place. And then came *the dress*. I never thought I'd like a mermaid-style dress, but the cut dissipated my sickly, sticklike appearance and allowed me to look like a somewhat normal person. This dress had a lace overlay, with pearls and beads on the top. It was pretty, feminine, and perfect! We added cap sleeves and a veil and voila!—I knew it was the dress, with my three supporters standing there, smiling, vigorously nodding their heads yes in agreement.

So five months later, on a gorgeous, sunny day, I donned my beautiful wedding gown. I, at roughly eighty two pounds, with pixie short (yet feminine-looking) hair—another huge answer to prayer!—walked down the aisle, eager to unite with the love of my life. Brother Donovan gave an introduction and then a short salvation sermon. Tyler, who God had blessed with an incredible voice, sang a song he had written for me for our wedding day. I hadn't heard it until that day. He entitled it "Never Let Go." My eyes were brimmed with tears, and then they spilled over onto my cheeks as he sang about his love for me and about me being the girl of *his* dreams. Me, who he had seen in all of my sickly state. I thought again about how he stayed right by my side. And now, here he was, my handsome prince charming, lovingly looking into my eyes as he promised to love me forever—to never let go. I won't ever forget that glorious moment.

I could feel the Lord's presence in the building as we said our vows to one another, exchanged rings, and were pronounced man and wife. We then, for the first time, walked down the aisle as Mr. and Mrs. Tyler Campbell! I was filled with such radiant happiness, such pure joy, and such deep love for my new husband! I also felt such love and gratefulness to my Lord and Savior, Jesus Christ, for giving me renewed life. He turned my life around, giving me what the Bible describes perfectly as "beauty for ashes" (Isaiah 61:3b) for giving me not only a wedding wonder but also a new life, happier than I ever could have dreamed.

A Furry Friend

A righteous man regardeth the life of his beast. (Proverbs 12:10a)

I loved (and still love) being married to Ty. We had a lot of fun together. We laughed a lot, talked a lot, and just enjoyed one another. It was hard for me to be all alone during the day while he was at work, though. For the first seven months of our marriage, I remained on maintenance chemo. This chemo consisted of only one of the five chemicals I had received during my aggressive chemotherapy treatments. Although I didn't get as sick, I couldn't get well and regain my strength very easily, either. I still had to spend the majority of my time in bed.

I relished the time we had together in the evenings, though. Then, in early September, Bible classes resumed. Class lasted from approximately 6:00–10:00 p.m., Monday through Thursday. I felt very thankful that Ty stayed committed to what the Lord wanted him to do, but I also missed him tremendously. I stayed too sick to go anywhere or do anything, and I remember feeling very isolated and lonely. But once again, the Lord proved his faithfulness and kindness by supplying me with a furry little friend.

Ty and I discussed getting a dog, but they could be pretty expensive, and we weren't sure if we should get one or not. So, we committed this desire to prayer. One week later (I'm stilled amazed by the quick timeline), Tyler's Aunt Lynne called. She bred full-blooded, registered Yorkies. The runt of the litter almost died just after birth, but Aunt Lynne nursed her back to health. This little puppy never had her tail docked, either, because she was so weak. Our tender-hearted aunt couldn't bring herself to sell this puppy to just anybody—she had to have just the right home for her. Ty's mom told her that we wanted a dog, and just like that, she said she'd give her to us as a gift. Praise the Lord, within two months, the Lord provided us with a beautiful, adorable little puppy. I got to decide her first name, and chose the name Anastasia, sometimes calling her Ana for short. Ty chose her middle name: Warchild. So, Anastasia Warchild Campbell became a new member of our family.

I loved our little Anastasia. She drastically brightened my days. If I needed to spend all day lying in bed, she laid down right next to me the whole time. Then, when Ty came home and wanted to throw her around and play more aggressively, she scampered about, enjoying the change of pace.

The Lord used her to motivate me to get out of bed. I took her outside to go potty at least twice a day, and made sure to take her on a short walk as well (this walk consisted of us circling the outside of the house at least one time). The Lord also used my little puppy to discover an immense improvement in my health. I previously mentioned that I had lost my ability to run or skip. One day, while taking Anastasia for our routine walk around the house, I suddenly wondered if I'd be able to jog instead. So off I went, with Anastasia happily trotting along beside me. I remember feeling like I would burst with joy. I could run again! I was really getting better! Praise God—he is so merciful! What a special, miraculous realization! And the Lord knew exactly what I needed to propel me into motion—a wonderful, lovable, furry friend.

28

For This Child I Prayed

He maketh the barren woman to keep house, and to be a
joyful mother of children. Praise ye the LORD. (Psalm 113:9)

I wanted children so badly. Ever since I could remember, I wanted
to be a wife and mommy. The thought of not being able to bear
children consistently brought tears to my eyes. I remember one
occasion when a lady in church handed her newborn baby to me
to hold. As I held her infant in my arms, tears instantly sprung
up in my eyes. I ducked my head and resisted the urge to quickly
thrust the baby back at her mother. I left, shocked by my strong
reaction and the instant, deep sadness I felt at the thought of not
being able to have a baby.

I remember Ty and I prayed together every day for a long
time, both during and after cancer, that the Lord would please
protect my body and allow us to have children. I received
Rotuxan (my maintenance chemo) intravenously every month,
and, as I've mentioned previously, although I didn't get as sick,
I still felt very ill. Ty never complained about how sick I stayed.
He just loved me, took care of me, and made me feel like the
most blessed girl in the world. I thanked the Lord for such a
wonderful husband, and earnestly prayed the Lord would let
me give him children.

Finally, seven months after our marriage, I had my very last dose of maintenance chemo in February of 2013.

Tyler graduated from Bible school in late May of 2013, and we moved to Colorado two days later to help with his dad's church. The Lord allowed us to be active in several church ministries, but I still struggled with my health. But the Lord didn't leave me in dire straits, and slowly but surely, my health improved. I started juicing again (I had stopped for a while) to try to detox my body from the chemotherapy and improve my nutrition.

I started feeling healthier and more energized, and then, out of nowhere, I began to feel *very hungry*. I remember being able to tell that something felt different, and I wondered if I could be pregnant. On January 25, 2014, just under one year after my last dose of maintenance chemo, we found out I was expecting! The Lord did "exceeding abundantly above all that we could ask or think" (Ephesians 3:20). Ty and I both wept with joy over our miracle. The Lord gave me a good, safe pregnancy—I wasn't high risk, nor did I have any complications.

On October 8, 2014, I gave birth to a beautiful, healthy baby boy. We named him David. We both cried at the sight of our little seven pound, two ounce miracle. I had never held anything more precious or flawless in my arms. I know exactly what Hannah (in the Bible) meant when she said in 1 Samuel 1:27, "For this child I prayed; and the LORD hath given me my petition which I asked of him." We prayed for our little David, and the Lord graciously granted us our petition.

When David was fifteen months old, we found out, miracle of miracles, that I was expecting again! We were overcome with joy by God's goodness and mercy. I gave birth to a second little son. We named him William. William was born on December 21, 2016, weighing six pounds, twelve ounces. Tears streamed down our faces as I held our second precious, adorable little miracle baby. Like David, he was absolutely perfect. I must tell you, dear reader, a very special blessing the Lord gave us in the timing of William's birth. If you remember, Tyler proposed to me on December 21, 2011. When Ty proposed to me, he mentioned, "I think of my preaching up here and looking down at you, and maybe a few other little Campbells ..." What a blessing for the Lord to allow me to give Tyler another little Campbell on the anniversary of his proposal! I truly cannot express to you how deep of a blessing that is!

I'm overcome with joy and the blessings of God's tender mercies. I cannot tell you how grateful and thankful I am to the Lord for giving me "the desires of my heart" (Psalm 37:4). He has caused "the barren woman to keep house, and to be a joyful mother of children" (Psalm 113:9).

29

Journeying to the Mission Field: The Scottish Scene

Pray ye therefore the Lord of the harvest, that he will send forth labourers into his harvest. (Matthew 9:38)

Here am I; send me. (Isaiah 6:8b)

I have always wanted to be a missionary. I desperately wanted to take the gospel of Jesus Christ to a people who didn't hear or know it. I wanted to help others and make a difference in their lives. My burden always remained very strong. But nobody I had dated ever felt called to the mission field. I knew that, as a wife, my calling would automatically be whatever call the Lord put on my husband's life. According to the Bible, he would be my head (Ephesians 5:23), and I would be "an help meet *for him*" (Genesis 2:18c, my emphasis) in whatever the Lord called him to do. After all, the Bible further explains, "Neither was the man created for the woman; but the woman for the man" (1 Corinthians 11:9). So I began to think the Lord just didn't plan for me to be a missionary.

Even while Ty and I dated, he never brought up feeling called to be a missionary, and I never mentioned wanting to be one. I didn't want to influence him—it was too big of a decision. Then, one night after class at Bible school (before I had cancer), Ty came out to my car, knelt down by my window, and said, "I think the Lord is calling me to be a missionary. Maybe he's just testing me to see if I'm willing, but I really think I'm actually called to be one." He looked at me somewhat hesitantly as he told me the news, not knowing how I would react.

My hand flew to my chest as I smiled from ear to ear. My eyes filled with tears as I burst, "I've always wanted to be a missionary! That's *great*!"

He grinned back at me, "You never said anything about it."

"That's because I didn't want to influence you!" I gushed. "I'm so happy!"

He began praying about where the Lord wanted him to go, and I prayed too. But he didn't get any specific direction about where to go. That summer, on August 6, 2011, we found out I had cancer. During the course of my cancer, Ty said he felt the burden to be a missionary lift off of him. He thinks it's because my health became so fragile, the Lord knew he couldn't handle thinking about going to the mission field in addition to my having cancer. But then, miraculously, the Lord allowed me to get better. My maintenance chemo ended four months before Ty graduated from Bible school. During his last year of Bible school, the Lord clearly directed us to move to Divide, Colorado, to help out his dad's church for a little while. We both knew this was a transitional call—that it was training for whatever the Lord had for us to do/where he had for us to be more permanently in the future. Ty led music, taught Sunday school class, and preached frequently. We both worked with the youth group. Then our church had its first missions conference. All the missionaries were such a blessing! The Lord really pricked our hearts. I knew we were called to go to the mission field. I surrendered to go, by God's grace, *anywhere* that he wanted us to go. I felt covered in "the peace of God, which passeth all understanding" (Philippians 4:7a). I knew the Lord could be trusted, and that the safest place to be was the center of his will—wherever that ended up being.

Ty also spent a long time praying at the altar. When he got back to our seat, he whispered in my ear, "We're called to be missionaries." I smiled, nodded my head, and hugged him. We both wept, feeling an overwhelming sense of peace and joy over our new call. We prayed for several months about where to go—especially about Africa and South America. Ty tried to set up a survey trip to Africa (a survey trip is when you go on a mission trip specifically to survey the country and see if that's where the Lord wants you to go permanently). But the Lord shut the door, and kept shutting doors about Africa.

On and off over the years, even before Ty and I met, I felt burdened for the people of Scotland. I prayed for them to hear the gospel and get saved. I never knew why I randomly thought of them—I never thought I'd go there as a missionary. But I just felt the need to pray for them.

Then one day, at the end of Tyler and I taking the youth group on an activity (this was several months after our missions conference), we met an elderly couple in the parking lot of a sports store. The woman spoke with a thick Irish accent and showed great excitement over our last name being Campbell. "Oh, Campbell—a good Scottish name!" she exclaimed. Her statement stood out to both of us.

The next day, as Ty was doing his daily Bible reading (he'd specifically been praying about the mission field too), some verses in Ezekiel chapter three really stood out to him. He said it felt like the Lord hit him right between the eyes, making him think, "Scotland!" Of course, I didn't have any idea about this, and when he came back upstairs to our room (I had been reading my Bible in our room), I randomly asked, "Have you ever thought about Scotland?"

"That's really funny you should say that ..." he responded, and then proceeded to tell me about his Bible reading. We both prayed about going to Scotland. That night, we had Wednesday night prayer meeting at church. Ty always read the missionary letters. That particular Wednesday, however, we only had one missionary letter. It was from our missionaries in (you'll never guess where …) *Scotland*. And in their prayer letter, they were asking for help! The Lord's timing is so perfect and specific. Tyler was in between jobs at the time, and in about three weeks, there was a new job that was supposed to open up for him. We both knew that if he started a new job, it would take at least one year to save up enough time to go on a mission trip. We both realized we'd have to try to plan a mission trip immediately, if possible. There was just enough of an open window of time. In addition, Ty and I had just filed our taxes. With the money we received back from our income tax return, we'd have enough money to afford the airfare and other expenses. David was almost four months old, so all of us could go as a family.

We both felt the Lord working, so we e-mailed our missionaries to Scotland (the Vogelpohl family) that night. We explained the situation and asked if there'd be a good time for us to visit—either immediately, since our schedule would allow that, or later on. We emphasized that we knew this was short notice, and if the timing didn't work for them for the immediate future, we would love to come some other time. Happily, we had both met the Vogelpohls, but on separate occasions, years earlier—before Ty and I had even met. I had met them when they were in Bible school in Florida (since I lived there so long). Tyler had met them in Colorado (when he was a young teen) a few years later, when they were trying to get to Scotland.

And now comes a series of events that only the Lord could orchestrate so smoothly and perfectly; I feel I must give you the details of our whirlwind experience. Early the next morning (Thursday morning), we received the Vogelpohls' reply: they remembered exactly who we were (they'd even prayed for me when I'd had cancer), and no time was too soon to come. They'd love to have us. Ty and I both sat in shock, not believing how suddenly everything seemed to be coming together. We e-mailed them back, asking about visiting from February fifth through the nineteenth (it was the very end of January). "Yes! Yes! Come! That timing would be perfect," was their response. Then suddenly we had to put on the brakes, realizing Tyler and David didn't have passports and mine was still in my maiden name. Talk about feeling deflated! Ty said, "Well, let's just go to the post office today and apply for our passports. We'll see what the Lord does."

We knew that it normally took four to six weeks to obtain a passport. We prayed the Lord would give us just the right person to help us and work out the timing. A kind older man gave us our applications, and when we explained our situation and that we wanted to do mission work, he immediately brightened. He was a Christian, and, wanting to help us just like we'd prayed, he told us to go to Aurora, Colorado, which is just outside of Denver, two hours away from where we lived. He said that they could expedite our passports in a few days' time (it was one of the two places in the United States that a passport could be expedited that quickly). But there was a catch: we needed to purchase our tickets *before* we went to the office, show our itinerary of how soon we'd leave the country, and plead our case for our passports. We also had to make an appointment with them before we arrived there.

We looked at the prices of plane tickets to Scotland for leaving in less than one week, and, to put it delicately, they were expensive! I felt a little worried, but my wonderful husband said, "Babe, I really believe the Lord has worked all of this out so far, and that he wants us to do this. Let's just stick out our neck and money for the Lord! He's worth it!" I instantly agreed, and we booked our flights for Tuesday, February 5, which meant we'd scheduled ourselves to leave in five days. We couldn't get an appointment with the passport office, but read from reviews online that they'd take you anyway.

The next morning, Friday, January 31, 2015, we drove the two hours to Aurora, Colorado, flight itineraries and other necessary paperwork in hand. We again prayed for just the right person. The

Lord answered our prayer! A young woman saw us—without an appointment!—and when we showed her our itineraries, she said they could have our passports ready for us in three days. The Lord put it on my heart to tell her that we lived two hours away, and she said, "Oh, well, in that case, since you live so far away, come back in a few hours, and we'll have them printed out for you."

Our jaws dropped and our hearts sang. What were the odds of that happening? We met with that lady at 10:30 a.m., and at 2:00 p.m., we came back and received three hot-off-the-presses passports. The Lord is just unbelievable in how he works out circumstances when he wants something to happen!

The Scottish Scene: So, we left for Scotland on February 5, 2015. During our visit, the Lord made our call to Scotland abundantly clear. The need for the gospel there is overwhelming. Many Scots today are atheists (don't believe in God/that there is a God), which I didn't know before. The population in Scotland, according to a 2011 census, is around 5.3 million (www.scotland.org). I always pictured Scotland as a quiet country with small villages and people milling about here and there. But Scotland is the exact opposite. It is literally teeming with people. Scotland has something called *high streets*. These high streets consist of cobblestone streets that span about fifty yards wide, are miles and miles long, and consist of only foot traffic. This means there aren't any cars on these streets, but rather throngs of people walking from point A to point B, going to grocery stores, department stores, bakeries— you name it. We visited in the coldest time of year, and there were still literally thousands of people out and about. Dane and Angie Vogelpohl told us that in the summer, you walk shoulder-to-shoulder with the many people who are there.

People from all over the world have come to live in Scotland, making it a large international hub of varying cultures. On our survey trip, we were able to pass out thousands of gospel tracts (literature that explains the gospel of Jesus Christ: "For Christ also hath once suffered for sins, the just for the unjust, that he might bring us to God, being put to death in the flesh, but quickened by the Spirit" I Peter 3:18). While we were there, Dane Vogelpohl (the missionary) talked to a Scottish man named Liam about the Lord and salvation through Jesus Christ. He realized his need to become born again and got saved (asked Jesus Christ to come into his heart, by faith, to wash away his sin and be his personal Savior)!

But when Dane first started talking to Liam about the Lord, he mentioned being a sinner. Liam said, "I don't know what that word means."

Dane explained, "You know, sin—If you've ever sinned before."

To which Liam confessed, "I don't know what sin is." So Dane explained sin to him (anything you do that's wrong is sin). His complete lack of knowledge of sin and the gospel shocked and saddened Tyler and me, and throughout our trip, we consistently realized that many people there have never heard the gospel before—have never had the opportunity to be introduced to Jesus Christ and to learn of and accept the sacrifice he made by dying on the cross as payment for their sins.

When we arrived back in the States two weeks later, we felt we'd left a part of our hearts in Scotland. We can't wait to get back there permanently, Lord willing, as missionaries. We want so desperately to reach the people of Scotland and tell them the good news of the gospel of Jesus Christ. We want to make a difference in their lives.

Currently Tyler, David, William, and I are trying to get to the mission field of Scotland. We're on something called *deputation*. This is where we travel all over the United States, visiting churches to raise support to get to Scotland (it's illegal for Tyler to get a job there under a ministerial visa, so you have to get sponsors [monthly supporters] through churches and/or individuals). We show each church the ministry we participated in when we were in Scotland, as well as the ministry we believe the Lord has for us to do once we move there permanently. It has been a journey with many joys and trials and is, overall, one big adventure. We plan to be in Scotland, Lord willing, in 2018, and are excited beyond words for this next chapter of our lives!

I often think about how drastically the Lord has changed my life! I, this once extremely ill, ever-so-tiny cancer patient, now, by God's grace, have the strength and health to travel all over the United States and beyond! I've been to Wyoming, Alaska, California, New York, and many other states. We've even gone to Canada! I never could have imagined, when I spent day after day and night after night trapped in a bed, that the Lord would give me such a rich, fulfilling life beyond "the valley of the shadow of death" (Psalm 23:4) that loomed over me.

The Lord has given me new life, dear reader. He spared my life from almost certain death with my case of cancer. He gave me a wonderful husband who I love so dearly, I cannot adequately express it to you in words. He enabled us to have our adorable little sons, who I was told were impossible to have, and who I now can't imagine life without. He's granted the desire I've had since childhood to be a missionary, allowing us to embark on an adventure I had only ever dreamed about. I know life will still have many trials and hardships. Not everything will be a bed of roses. But I have learned and seen God's faithfulness and kindness. He can be trusted in the best and worst of circumstances. I want, more than anything else, dear reader, to take this life the Lord has given me, and give it back to Him. I don't want to waste what the Lord has given me. I owe him everything, and more than anything, I want my life to bring glory to my Savior, Jesus Christ. I am the result of his grace, comfort, and, most of all, his tender mercies.

30

What a Friend We Have in Jesus

There is a friend that sticketh closer than
a brother. (Proverbs 18:24b)

I would love to tell you what I think of Jesus, since
I found in Him a friend so strong and true; I would
tell you how he changed my life completely, He did
something that no other Friend could do ...
—"No One Ever Cared For Me Like Jesus,"
a hymn by Dr. Charles Weigle, 1991

I hope I've been able to convey to you, my dear reader, what a
faithful, invaluable friend Jesus Christ has been to me. He is
my very best friend. I love him so dearly—he saved my life
from the scary grip of cancer. But even more deeply than that, I've
received him as my personal Savior. I have committed and trust
my very soul to Jesus Christ.

As time has passed, and the Lord has given me the ability
to talk to others about him, I've found a common pattern. Many
people haven't been told how to have Jesus Christ live in their
heart forever—to *know* that they have *eternal life* in heaven after
they die: "These things have I written unto you that believe on
the name of the Son of God; that ye may *know* that ye have *eternal*

life, and that ye may believe on the name of the Son of God" (1 John 5:13, my emphasis). And not just life in eternity, but *new life*, joy, peace, and hope *in this present life as well*. "Therefore if any man be in Christ, he is a new creature: old things are passed away; behold, all things are become new" (2 Corinthians 5:17). Let me tell you the way to Jesus Christ.

It's very simple. You must believe that Jesus Christ, God's Son, died on the cross and shed his blood as the payment for your sins. And you must pray and ask him, by faith (plus nothing else), to come into your heart to be your personal Savior. I have my own personal testimony of how I became saved/born again (I'll explain this phrase in more detail later): "Jesus answered ... Except a man be born again, he cannot see the kingdom of God ... Ye must be born again" (John 3:3, 7).

I knew I was a sinner ... that I had done wrong things—"all unrighteousness is sin" (I John 5:17a). Anything someone does that isn't right is sin, according to the Bible. I knew I wasn't as good as God and never could be: "For all have sinned, and come short of the glory of God" (Romans 3:23). "All our righteousnesses (good works) are as filthy rags" (before God) (Isaiah 64:6b). I also knew that, even if I was a really good person (and I try to be), I couldn't get to heaven on account of my good works/being a good person. The Bible specifically states, about getting to heaven, "Not of works, lest any man should boast" (Ephesians 2:9).

Ah, but God's wonderful mercy poured out through the sacrifice of Jesus Christ dying on the cross and shedding his blood *to pay for my sins*. He was sinless (just), whereas I wasn't sinless, and therefore unjust. This verse summed up what Jesus did for you and me perfectly: "For Christ also hath once suffered for sins, the just (Christ) for the unjust (me and any other sinner), that he might bring us to God, being put to death in the flesh (dying on the cross), but quickened (raised from the dead) by the Spirit" (1 Peter 3:18). I believed with all my heart that Jesus Christ is God's Son, and that he died on the cross to pay for my sin. "Behold the

Lamb of God (Jesus), which taketh away the sin of the world" (John 1:29b). I knew I wasn't good enough to get to heaven and that I needed to simply pray and ask Jesus, by faith, to come into my heart to be my personal Savior. "That if thou shalt confess with thy mouth the Lord Jesus, and shalt believe in thine heart that God hath raised him from the dead, thou shalt be saved" (Romans 10:9). So I did.

I prayed something like this: "Dear Lord, I know I am a sinner, and I believe that Jesus died on the cross for my sins. I'm asking you, by faith, to please come into my heart and save me and be my personal Savior. In Jesus's name, Amen." I prayed to be saved and be born again when I was eleven years old. Actually, I vaguely remember praying to be saved when I was four, but it's not a very clear memory. I don't know for sure if I understood what I was doing or not. So I prayed again when I was eleven because this time I was sure I understood what I was doing and would forever have a very clear memory of the day I prayed to be saved.

The other side of not being born again is spending eternity in hell ... and I believe I would be committing an atrocity to you, dear reader, to omit what awaits a soul that isn't "written in the book of life" (Revelation 20:15). The Bible says about hell, "And whosoever was not found written in the book of life was cast into the lake of fire" (Revelation 20:15). It's a literal eternal fire where "the smoke of their torment ascendeth up forever and ever" (Revelation 14:11a). But the wonderful aspect about hell is that *nobody has to go there.* God is "not willing that any should perish, but that all should come to repentance" (2 Peter 3:9c).

The Bible says, "Behold, now is the accepted time; behold, now is the day of salvation" (2 Corinthians 6:2b). The Lord takes special care to mention "now" being the "day" of salvation. Salvation is not a lifelong journey. It is an *event* that takes place the instant a person/sinner asks Jesus to save his or her soul (just like the event of being born—thus the phrase "born again"). I have met many people who believe in God and Jesus Christ. A lot of them said they had prayed to God for help or asked him to forgive them when they did something wrong (sinned). But many of them admitted there had never been a time when they actually *asked Jesus to come into their hearts to be their Savior*. Often the reason they hadn't was because *no one ever explained to them that that's how to get saved and go to heaven (not hell) when they died*. They just didn't know.

I want to share with you an analogy that made perfect sense to me about getting saved/being born again: Say you are $300,000 in debt (your debt is now due to be paid in full), and you don't have the money to pay your debt. Then someone, who you know is very wealthy and could easily cover your bill, says to you, "I heard about your situation, and I want to help you. I wrote a check out to you for the full amount you owe, and I left it in an envelope at the post office with your name on it. All you have to do is take the check, cash it, and your debt will be paid." Okay. So, say you *know* that this person has the money to cover all of your debt, and you *believe* them that they wrote out the check for you (made the payment for you) and left it at the post office. *But*, if there's never been a time that *you personally* have gone to the post office, picked up the check, and *cashed* it, then is your bill/debt paid or not? *It's not*. It's the same thing with being born again and asking Jesus to save you!!

Please, my dear reader, if you can't recall a time that you've specifically prayed and asked Jesus Christ to come into your heart *by faith alone* ("For by grace are ye saved through faith ..." Ephesians 2:8a) to be your Savior, pray and ask him to come into your heart and save you today! "For whosoever shall call upon the name of the Lord shall be saved" (Romans 10:13). Will you do that right now? It's the best decision you'll ever make!! You will *know* that you're going to heaven and not hell when you die, and you'll have Jesus Christ with you to love you and help you during every minute of every day for the rest of your life. "I will never leave thee, nor forsake thee" (Hebrews 13:5b).

Discover, like I have, what a friend we have in Jesus.

"No one ever cared for me like Jesus. There's no other Friend so kind as he. No one else could take the sin and darkness from me. Oh how much he cares for me!"
—"No One Ever Cared For Me Like Jesus,"
a hymn by Dr. Charles Weigle, 1991

Tips for Cancer

Ointment and perfume rejoice the heart: so doth the sweetness
of a man's friend by hearty counsel. (Proverbs 27:9)

1) Stay cool and comfortable. If you get too hot, it's very easy
to become dehydrated. For me, getting dehydrated resulted in my
being in more pain as well as vomiting repeatedly until I had to
go to the hospital for fluids. Many times, they admitted me as a
result of the extreme dehydration. Be aware that *you can become
dehydrated very quickly.*

2) Zophran is a wonderful anti-nausea pill. It can, however, cause
painful hiccups. Your body will eventually adjust, though. It also
affects your GI track, so it's necessary to take something to offset
those symptoms. But, for me at least, it was the best anti-nausea
medication I took.

3) Talk to your doctor about your symptoms! Sometimes the
symptoms you're experiencing are either abnormal or more severe
than they should be. Dr. Collins (my oncologist) helped me many times
by adjusting my medication or chemo. You may be in unnecessary
discomfort. Also, you don't know as much as or more than your
doctor! *Talk to your doctor.* I'm not saying a doctor can never be
wrong, so pray for the Lord to give them (and you) wisdom to make
the right decisions for you. But the Lord put your doctor there for you.

4) Another oncologist told me to **take 50,000IUs of liquid vitamin D3 every day** (you can buy this at a local health food store or online). Vitamin D3 helps with building and supporting your immune system. There were a few times I came into contact with contagious people, but I believe the Lord used the vitamin D3 to prevent me from getting their illness (chemo devastates your immune system). I also noticed that vitamin D3 helped with my energy and moods. Dr. Collins told me that people who have lymphoma are deficient/low in vitamin D. I noticed, both during and after cancer, a vast, negative difference if I stopped taking my vitamin D3.

5) Rest! I understand the frustration (to put it very lightly) of being limited. But your body is in a battle and not operating under normal conditions or circumstances. Rest allows your body to regroup and fight more effectively. If you push your limits, you'll most likely end up feeling and getting very sick—trust me, I know.

6) I juiced both during and after cancer. Laura kept trying different concoctions to see which one tasted the best—and she always tasted it first! I juiced once a day, drinking approximately eight ounces (we built up to this—I started off with about two ounces).

This was the winning **recipe:** 1 apple (can substitute with a pear), 3–4 organic carrots, 1/4 beet, 1/4–1/2 of a cucumber (can substitute with zucchini), 2 stalks of celery, 1 large handful of spinach. I prefer a juicer that has filters, as the juice is smooth with no pulp. Put the spinach in first since it doesn't yield much juice. **If you want fewer ingredients** because of expense or convenience, I sometimes limited my recipe to the apple, beets, carrots, and celery. It's best to use organic produce. **Rinse/wash the fruit and vegetables thoroughly.** Laura usually added my vitamin D3 to my juice. **You want to drink the juice within**

thirty minutes of it being made. After thirty minutes, the potency reduces a great deal. You can also look up juicing recipes online that include ingredients that will be most beneficial to your specific type of cancer.

7) Try to eat lots of green vegetables if you're able. They're healthy, help with digestion/constipation, and help to reduce the acidity in your system (thus making your body more alkaline).

8) Try to avoid or reduce sugar—especially refined sugar. Attempt to find/use substitutes such as honey, stevia, maple syrup, agave nectar, coconut sugar, or unrefined sugar. You don't have to drive yourself crazy about it, though. You must eat, and if the only thing you can bear to eat is sugary, then go for it! I have a sweet tooth, so I tried to mainly avoid refined sugar and limit my other sugar intake. Although there are differing opinions about whether or not sugar feeds cancer, I feel pretty confident that sugar does feed cancer (at least to some extent). This is why: when one has a PET scan to see where the cancer is, the technician gives you **radioactive glucose (sugar)** to either drink or receive intravenously. **The cancer flocks to the sugar and feeds on it,** and therefore lights up because the glucose is radioactive. If cancer doesn't love sugar, in my mind, the cancerous cells wouldn't quickly and suddenly devour it.

9) Although it's best to eat healthy, it's not always doable on chemotherapy. Your taste buds and appetite will be weird and sometimes non-existent. If a certain food or dish didn't sound good to me but I still ate it, I threw it up. Your body needs nourishment and fuel to combat the cancer and stand the chemotherapy and/or radiation. So if most of what you eat is junk, so be it! One time, I became so concerned with eating only healthy foods, I stopped eating anything remotely unhealthy. But, I couldn't stomach the healthy food, so for two to three days, I barely ate anything. Ty,

Mrs. Donovan, and Laura all gave me pep talks, encouraging me to eat what I could, and if it wasn't healthy, that was okay. I began eating my not-entirely-healthy food (i.e.: fried chicken), but felt much better and stronger from the nourishment.

10) I took a supplement called Perfect Food, Super Green Formula. It's in pill form (they also have it in powder form), and the brand is Garden of Life. I struggled to eat enough greens/vegetables, so this helped as a whole food supplement. If I had sugar or unhealthy foods, I felt comforted that I at least had something healthy in my Perfect Food pill as well as my juicing regimen. Start off with half a pill per day. I eventually worked up to two pills per day. Don't take it at night, as it will keep you wide awake for hours!

11) When you're in pain, watching light movies really helps. Don't be surprised if you stop being able to watch action movies or other movies you previously enjoyed. Sickness—especially cancer—changes what you can and can't tolerate.

12) Everybody's experience with cancer and chemotherapy (I never had to have radiation) **is different.** With my chemo and the aggressiveness of it, I couldn't read anymore (and I love to read). I didn't have the strength, health, or ability to concentrate; it just took too much effort. I forced myself to read at least one chapter of my Bible every day, but I also listened to the Bible on CD quite frequently. I would highly recommend doing that if you're unable to read.

13) Try to drink lots of water or fluids the day you've had chemo. Fluids help to flush the chemo and reduce the bad symptoms.

14) **If you're up to it, have visitors!** I found that social interaction really encouraged me. It's easy to feel very cut off and alienated from the rest of the world.

15) **Take your medication! Stay on top of your pain meds! Don't try to be a tough guy!** It's very important to stay on top of and/or ahead of your pain. Once the pain sets in, it's a lot harder and takes a much longer time to play catch up. I found this out the hard way.

16) **Be aware that your body may develop a food sensitivity from all the distress.** For example, I found out I developed either a food sensitivity or allergy to corn. I also can't tolerate pork of any kind now, and for a long time, I couldn't eat red meat. It was too hard on my stomach and made me sick. Thank the Lord, I can eat steak and all-beef hot dogs again now, although for some reason, I still don't feel well after eating hamburger meat.

17) **Try to have a thankful heart**, although I know that that can be very difficult. But your perspective makes a big difference. After all, the Bible says, "The spirit of a man will sustain his infirmity" (Proverbs 18:14a). Your morale is very important.

18) **I realized having cancer wasn't the end of the world.** It can be hard and discouraging at times, but the Lord is in control, not you. He makes the difference and brings meaningful, special blessings along the way.

19) **Take your journey one day at a time.** Don't worry about or focus on how many treatments you have left or how many more months you have to endure of being sick and limited. You'll quickly feel overwhelmed and discouraged. Live each day, and live *in* each day—not the one a week from now or a month from now. The Lord gives grace one day at a time.

20) I used to think that when a person's cancer was all gone, that meant that they were completely well. But that's not the case. The cancer is gone, but recovering from the aftermath of the treatments usually takes a very long time. They still need a lot of prayer for a long while! Also, most cancer patients, once they're well, don't reach the same level of physical wellness and ability that they had before cancer. And that's okay. There's nothing wrong or "wimpy" with having a new/different level of normal.

Tyler and I in the hospital after my first round of chemo

Ty taking me to dinner to debut my new haircut

Losing my hair, but not my hope

Sporting my new "turban" look

December 30, 2011, cancer free!

Bride and Groom two days before our wedding

My "Picture Perfect" painting from Dr. Ruckman

June 2, 2012, Mrs. Campbell at last!

Happy beyond belief!

My "knight in shining armor"

Ty and I, five years post cancer

Tyler, David, William, and I, summer of 2017

David, a feisty 3, and William, an exploring 7 month old

My mischievous little David

My contented "Baby Willum," as his big brother calls him

Me with my two little miracles

Printed in the United States
By Bookmasters